Great Meals in Minutes was created by
Rebus, Inc.
and published by Time-Life Books.

Rebus, Inc.

Publisher: Rodney Friedman
Editorial Director: Shirley Tomkievicz

Editor: Marya Dalrymple
Art Director: Ronald Gross
Managing Editor: Brenda Goldberg
Senior Editor: Charles Blackwell
Food Editor and Food Stylist: Grace Young
Photographer: Steven Mays
Prop Stylist: Cathryn Schwing
Staff Writer: Alexandra Greeley
Associate Editor: Ann M. Harvey
Assistant Editor: Bonnie J. Slotnick
Assistant Food Stylist: Karen Hatt
Photography Assistant: Glenn Maffei
Recipe Tester: Gina Palombi Barclay
Production Assistant: Lorna Bieber

For information about any Time-Life book,
please write:
Reader Information
Time-Life Books
541 North Fairbanks Court
Chicago, Illinois 60611

Library of Congress Cataloging in Publication Data
Turkey & duck menus.
  (Great meals in minutes)
  Includes index.
  1. Cookery (Turkeys)   2. Cookery (Ducks)
3. Menus.   4. Cooks—Biography.
  I. Title: Turkey and duck menus.   II. Series.
TX750.T87   1985   641.6′6592   84-28092
ISBN 0-86706-257-6 (lib. bdg.)
ISBN 0-86706-256-8 (retail ed.)

Time-Life Books Inc.
is a wholly owned subsidiary of
Time Incorporated

Founder: Henry R. Luce 1898–1967

Editor-in-Chief: Henry Anatole Grunwald
President: J. Richard Munro
Chairman of the Board: Ralph P. Davidson
Corporate Editor: Jason McManus
Group Vice President, Books: Reginald K.
Brack Jr.

Time-Life Books Inc.

Editor: George Constable
Executive Editor: George Daniels
Director of Design: Louis Klein
Board of Editors: Roberta Conlan,
Ellen Phillips, Gerry Schremp, Gerald
Simons, Rosalind Stubenberg, Kit van
Tulleken, Henry Woodhead
Editorial General Manager: Neal Goff
Director of Research: Phyllis K. Wise
Director of Photography: John Conrad Weiser

President: Reginald K. Brack Jr.
Senior Vice President: William Henry
Vice Presidents: George Artandi, Stephen L.
Bair, Robert A. Ellis, Juanita T. James,
Christopher T. Linen, James L. Mercer,
Joanne A. Pello, Paul R. Stewart

Editorial Operations
Design: Ellen Robling (assistant director)
Copy Room: Diane Ullius
Production: Ann B. Landry (director), Celia
Beattie
Quality Control: James J. Cox (director),
Sally Collins
Library: Louise D. Forstall

SERIES CONSULTANT
Margaret E. Happel is the author of *Ladies
Home Journal Adventures in Cooking,
Ladies Home Journal Handbook of Holiday
Cuisine,* and other best-selling cookbooks, as
well as the translator and adapter of Rebecca
Hsu Hiu Min's *Delights of Chinese Cooking.*
A food consultant based in New York City,
she has been director of the food department
of *Good Housekeeping* and editor of
American Home magazine.

WINE CONSULTANT
Tom Maresca combines a full-time career
teaching English literature with writing
about and consuming fine wines. He is now
at work on *The Wine Case Book,* which
explains the techniques of wine tasting.

Cover: Bruce Aidells's Creole-style duck with
dirty rice and bittersweet tossed salad.
See pages 91–93.

Great Meals
IN MINUTES

TURKEY & DUCK
MENUS

TIME-LIFE BOOKS, ALEXANDRIA, VIRGINIA

Contents

Meet the Cooks

VICKI CHEUNG

A native of Hong Kong, Vicki Cheung attended college in London, then moved to New York, where she graduated from the New York City Technical College with a degree in Hotel and Restaurant Technology and Management. Later, she worked as a food decorator at Le Cirque restaurant. She is currently a caterer and a freelance food stylist.

LESLIE LAND

Food writer and consultant Leslie Land, who now lives in Maine, was raised on a farm in Pennsylvania. She began her cooking career during college, when she worked as a part-time caterer. After college, she cooked at Chez Panisse in Berkeley, California. She writes a syndicated weekly food column and contributes articles to *Yankee* and *Food & Wine*.

DOUGLAS OAKS

Certified as an executive chef and culinary educator by the American Culinary Federation, Douglas Oaks has received numerous cooking awards, including top prizes in the ACF national culinary competition held annually in Chicago. He has trained in restaurants in Minneapolis and St. Paul and has studied cooking abroad. At present he is executive chef at Litton Microwave Cooking.

LESLEE REIS

Until Leslee Reis married, she had never cooked an entire meal. Today she is the owner and head chef of Café Provençal in Evanston, Illinois, and a partner in Leslee's, a casual restaurant, also in Evanston, that features eclectic American meals. She has worked as a caterer, a restaurant consultant, and a teacher of French cooking.

HOLLY GARRISON
Born in Reading, Pennsylvania, Holly Garrison has been interested in cooking and fine food for most of her life. Trained as a journalist, she also attended cooking classes in the United States and in Europe. She is the food editor of *Parents* magazine.

DANIÈLE DELPEUCH
Danièle Delpeuch was born in Paris and raised in the Périgord region of southwestern France, where she now lives on a farm that once belonged to her grandfather. In 1979 she created the Ecole d'Art et Traditions du Périgord, and in 1983 and 1984 toured the United States demonstrating the traditional cooking techniques of Périgord.

JENIFER HARVEY LANG
Food writer and professional cook Jenifer Harvey Lang trained at the Culinary Institute of America. After graduation, she served as chef at Nathan's, a northern Italian restaurant in Washington, D.C. Her food column, "Tastings," appears monthly in the United Airlines in-flight magazine, and she is the author of a rated guide to the forty most important staples in the American pantry.

BRUCE AIDELLS
Early in his cooking career, Californian Bruce Aidells ran an on-campus restaurant at the University of California at Santa Cruz. Later, he was executive chef for the Poulet restaurant in Berkeley, where he prepared poultry in more than 500 different ways. He is now a restaurant consultant and teaches Louisiana-style cooking at the California Culinary Academy in San Francisco.

JEANNE MARIE VOLTZ
Born in Mobile, Alabama, Jeanne Marie Voltz began her food career operating an executive dining room catering service in New York City. She was the president of Cary Kitchens, a food consulting firm. She now works freelance on numerous projects including television commercials, movies, and print advertisements.

Turkey & Duck Menus in Minutes

GREAT MEALS FOR FOUR IN AN HOUR OR LESS

While whole roast turkey and duck—with all the trimmings—will always be traditional holiday fare, many modern cooks have realized that these versatile birds can grace any season's table when they are halved, quartered, shredded, cubed, or finely ground. Thus, both turkey and duck lend themselves to any number of cooking methods—stir frying, sautéing, and roasting, to name a few—and are perfect meal solutions for busy cooks.

Native to the New World, wild turkeys were widely hunted by Indians of the Americas, including the Aztecs of Mexico, who had domesticated them by the sixteenth century. According to many historians, the Spanish conqueror of the Aztecs, Hernán Cortés, was the first European to taste turkey meat. Apparently he delighted in it so much that he took several of the live birds back to Spain. As French gastronome Anthelme Brillat-Savarin observed after a nineteenth-century American tour, "The turkey is certainly one of the handsomest gifts the New World made to the Old World. . . .[Cooked turkey] is charming to look at, delightful to smell, and delicious to taste."

Turkeys have figured prominently in American lore. For example, the Navajos tell of an enormous hen turkey that flew over their fields, bringing them corn and teaching them how to cultivate their crops. And Benjamin Franklin made no secret of his displeasure when the bald eagle was chosen over his proposed "original native" turkey as a national symbol. Contemporary records show that the Pilgrims actually did serve roast turkey at the first Thanksgiving feast in 1621, and today Americans continue to serve turkey on that holiday and increasingly throughout the year.

Thirty years ago, 90 percent of all turkey was sold during November and December, but in 1983, turkey sales during the winter months accounted for only 40 percent of the yearly total. In 1983 alone, Americans consumed 11.2 pounds of turkey per person. It is not difficult to understand the enthusiasm for this multi-use bird: Turkey parts cook quickly, cost relatively little per pound (on the average, 50 cents less than ground beef, 70 cents less than chicken breasts, and $1.50 less than pork chops), and are sold fresh or frozen in every supermarket. Moreover, turkey works well in ethnic and regional recipes like turkey tacos, curries, stir fries, hash, and pot pies.

Ducks were first domesticated by the Chinese more than 2,000 years ago. In the 1870s, an enterprising clipper-ship captain managed to bring nine Peking ducks (which were raised only in the Imperial Palace) to Long Island, and today's highly flavored, tender White Peking (or Long Island) ducks are their descendants.

In general ducks have not enjoyed the same prominence at the dinner table as other poultry has. Per capita consumption of domestic duck is only three-quarters of a pound—perhaps because duck has a lower ratio of edible meat to bone than chicken or turkey, or perhaps because the preparation and cooking of duck has intimidated many Americans. Recently, however, Americans have become increasingly aware that duck's rich meat is a perfect foil for many vegetable dishes and is delicious accompanied by tart fruits and seasonings. Many people are now beginning to realize that duck need not take hours to prepare.

Both turkey and duck play an important role in many of the world's cuisines. On the following pages, nine of America's most talented cooks present 27 complete menus, showing how these birds can be adapted to Hungarian, Italian, Chinese, Indian, American regional, Polish, Mexican, and French recipes. Each menu, which serves four people, can be prepared in an hour or less, and the cooks focus on a new kind of American cuisine that borrows ideas and techniques from around the world but also values our native traditions. They use fresh produce, with no powdered sauces or other dubious shortcuts. The other ingredients (vinegars, spices, herbs, and so on) are all of high quality and are widely available in supermarkets or specialty food stores.

The cooks and the kitchen staff have meticulously planned and tested the meals for appearance as well as taste, as the accompanying photographs show: The vegetables are brilliant and fresh, the visual combinations appetizing. The table settings feature bright colors, simple flower arrangements, and attractive but not necessarily expensive serving dishes.

For each menu, the Editors, with advice from the cooks, suggest wines and other beverages. And there are suggestions for the use of leftovers and for complementary dishes and desserts. On each menu page, you will find a

Halved, quartered, cubed, or ground, turkey and duck are excellent choices for busy cooks. On the stovetop, sautéed turkey with strips of green and red bell pepper. On the counter (clockwise from top right), fresh tarragon and rosemary, a tomato, shallots, kosher salt, a quartered duck, fresh oregano, garlic, a pepper, and some peppercorns.

Cooking at high temperatures will be less dangerous if you follow a few simple tips:

▶ Water added to hot fat will always cause spattering. If possible, pat foods dry with a cloth or paper towel before you add them to the hot oil.

▶ Place food gently into any pan containing hot fat, or the fat will spatter.

▶ If you are boiling or steaming some foods while sautéing others, place the pots on the stove top far enough apart so that the water is unlikely to splash into the hot fat.

▶ Turn pot handles inward, so that you do not accidentally knock over a pot containing hot foods or liquids.

▶ Remember that alcohol—wine, brandy, or spirits—may occasionally catch fire when you add it to a very hot pan. If this happens, step back for your own protection and quickly cover the pan with a lid. The fire will instantly subside, and the food will not be spoiled.

▶ Keep pot holders and mitts close enough to be handy while cooking, but *never* hang them over the burners or lay them on the stove top.

---

number of other tips, from an easy method for stuffing a turkey breast to advice for selecting fresh produce.

BEFORE YOU START
Great Meals in Minutes is designed for efficiency and ease. This book will work best for you if you follow these suggestions:

1. Read the following guidelines for selecting turkey and duck.

2. Refresh your memory with the few simple cooking techniques on the following pages. They will quickly become second nature and will help you to produce professional-quality meals in minutes.

3. Read the menus before you shop. Each lists the ingredients you will need, in the order that you would expect to shop for them. Many items will already be on your pantry shelf.

4. Check the equipment list on page 14. Good, sharp knives and pots and pans of the right shape and material are essential for making great meals in minutes. This may be the time to buy a few things. The right equipment can turn cooking from a necessity into a creative experience.

5. Set out everything you need before you start to cook. The lists at the beginning of each menu tell just what is required. To save effort, always keep your ingredients in the same place so you can reach for them instinctively.

6. Follow the start-to-finish steps for each menu. That way, you can be sure of having the entire meal ready to serve in an hour.

SELECTING TURKEY AND DUCK
For the recipes in this volume, you will need turkey and duck parts or ground turkey. Turkey parts are now widely available fresh and frozen at supermarkets and butchers; ducks are sold whole or as packaged breasts. If you cannot find parts or ground turkey, have a butcher prepare the turkey or duck for you, or do so yourself.

Official Inspection
Poultry, like meat, must be inspected for wholesomeness. Before a bird can be shipped across state lines, USDA inspectors must check that it comes from a healthy flock, has been killed under rigid sanitary conditions, contains no harmful chemicals or additives, and is properly packaged and labeled. Look for the circular inspection mark on the paper wing tag, giblet wrap, plastic overwrap, or insert card.

All major processors also have their poultry graded. The highest quality receives a Grade A shield, meaning that the bird is well shaped, meaty with a layer of fat, has no skin defects and no parts missing. Grades B and C indicate lower-quality birds, which are rarely sold at retail. Whole turkeys, turkey thighs, drumsticks, and wings are graded; whole ducks are graded but duck breasts are not. Look for grade marks near the inspection tags.

In the Market
Today's turkey, which has approximately 25 percent more meat on it than the turkey of 30 years ago, is bred for hardiness, disease resistance, and for a higher proportion of white meat to dark.

Select turkey parts with pearly white skin (not purplish or bluish) that is not broken or blemished. The pieces should look plump and meaty, feel firm, and be odor free. Frozen parts—if properly handled by the supplier—can be nearly as tender and juicy as fresh ones when cooked. If the frozen parts are wrapped in clear rather than opaque plastic, check the skin for color and appearance; if not, be sure the pieces have not begun to thaw. Check that there are no pinkish ice crystals around the meat; this means the parts have thawed and then been refrozen and that the meat will be stringy and tasteless when cooked. There should be no breaks in the wrapping. Unless you are planning to use the frozen parts within a day, put them into your freezer immediately.

Ground turkey is generally a mixture of dark and white meat unless labeled all dark. It is sold frozen and occasionally fresh at most supermarkets. A butcher will grind turkey for you; or you can grind boneless breast or roast turkey at home in a food processor or meat grinder.

Today, scientific breeding and advanced feeding methods are producing consistently plump and juicy ducks, which are available fresh from late spring through late winter at some butchers. Ducks are marketed at seven to twelve weeks of age, when they are still technically ducklings (they are usually labeled as such) weighing from 3 to 5½ pounds.

Select fresh duck that is broad breasted and well padded with fat. The skin should be elastic rather than flabby and should be clean and free of pinfeathers. The flesh should be off-white, not yellow like that of chicken. As with turkey, duck should be odor free. If you are buying packaged duck breast, avoid any package that has liquid at the bottom; this indicates the duck has been frozen and then thawed, or has been in the package too long. Because duck is fatty, it freezes well and retains its juiciness when thawed. In fact, 90 percent of the ducks sold in America are frozen. If you buy frozen duck, check that the bird is solidly frozen and that the wrapping is intact.

STORING TURKEY AND DUCK
To prevent the growth of harmful bacteria, keep all poultry well chilled before use, and handle properly. After working with raw poultry, rinse any cutting surfaces with cold water, then scrub with hot soapy water and air dry.

You can store fresh turkey or duck for up to three days in the refrigerator. Remove the wrapping, wipe the meat with paper towels, then wrap it loosely in plastic.

Freezing fresh poultry preserves its high quality. The quicker you get it into the freezer the better. Set the freezer temperature at 0 degrees or lower. Use only moistureproof and vaporproof material such as heavy-duty aluminum foil, coated freezer paper, or heavy-duty plastic freezer bags. Never use lightweight plastic produce bags; they are not vaporproof. When wrapping poultry, exclude as much air as possible to prevent freezer burn, then seal the packages with freezer tape. Place store-bought frozen turkey or duck in its original wrapper in the freezer until ready to thaw for cooking. Frozen whole turkeys keep well for up to a year; turkey parts for six months; whole ducks and duck parts for several months. Label each package with the date. Once thawed, treat the poultry as you would fresh poultry, and do not refreeze it until it is cooked.

Storing cooked turkey and duck is simple and safe provided you follow a few basic tips. Cool the meat quickly, remove it from the bones, if desired, then wrap it in foil or place it in a covered plastic container. Keep it in the coldest part of the refrigerator, and eat it within three to four days. To freeze cooked poultry, follow the wrapping instructions above, and use the meat within two months. Once thawed, it must never be refrozen.

PREPARING TURKEY AND DUCK FOR COOKING
The thawing time for a frozen turkey or duck depends on its size and how you choose to thaw it. One method is to place the frozen poultry in its wrapping on a plate or in a pan in the refrigerator. A whole bird takes from one to three days to thaw this way; turkey breasts, depending on size, need a full day; turkey parts thaw in 2 to 2½ hours; and a 3- to 5½-pound duck takes 24 to 36 hours.

A second method requires that the poultry, in a watertight wrapping, be completely submerged in cold water (warm water will cause the outside of the bird to thaw too quickly and can cause the proliferation of bacteria).

Change the cold water every 30 minutes. This method thaws a 3- to 5½-pound duck in 2 to 3 hours and an 8- to 12-pound turkey in 4 to 6 hours. Never thaw poultry at room temperature.

Before cooking a fresh or thawed turkey or duck, check that all the pinfeathers are removed, or singe off any that remain. Finally, briefly rinse the poultry under cold water, dry it thoroughly, and cut into parts, if required.

GENERAL COOKING TECHNIQUES
Sautéing
Sautéing is a form of quick frying, with no cover on the pan. In French, *sauter* means "to jump," which is what vegetables or small pieces of food do when you shake the sauté pan. The purpose is to brown the food lightly and seal in the juices, sometimes before further cooking. This technique has three critical elements: the right pan, the proper temperature, and dry food.

The sauté pan: A proper sauté pan is 10 to 12 inches in diameter and has 2- to 3-inch straight sides that allow you to turn the food and still keep the fat from spattering. It has a heavy bottom that can be moved back and forth across a burner.

The best material (and the most expensive) for a sauté pan is tin-lined copper because it is a superior heat conductor. Heavy-gauge aluminum works well but will discolor acidic food like tomatoes. Therefore, you should not use aluminum if acidic food is to be cooked for more than 20 minutes after the initial browning. Another option is to select a heavy-duty sauté pan made of strong, heat-conducting aluminum alloys. This type of professional cookware is smooth and stick resistant.

Use a sauté pan large enough to hold the food without

Duck Fat

A tasty cooking medium, duck fat is used in a number of recipes in this volume. You can purchase rendered duck fat at a butcher shop that sells fresh duck or you can render it yourself using the fat taken from a fresh or defrosted duck. Rendering fat also produces cracklings—crunchy, flavorful brown bits that can be eaten like popcorn or incorporated into a recipe. Holly Garrison has her own method for preparing duck skin cracklings on page 63.

The method below can be used for rendering fat from any type of poultry.

1. Remove all fat and skin. Dice fat and skin and place in heavy-gauge saucepan with enough cold water to cover.

2. Over low heat, bring the water to a simmer and cook slowly, stirring occasionally, about 15 minutes, or until the fat is completely melted, the water has evaporated, and the cracklings are crisp.

3. Line a strainer or sieve with damp cheesecloth. Pour the liquid fat through the cheesecloth, reserving the cracklings.

4. If the cracklings are not crisp enough, return them to the pan and brown a bit longer, watching carefully to make sure they don't burn.

Disjointing a Duck

Disjointing a whole duck takes only minutes and produces 8 or 10 pieces (4 with breast meat) that you can cook quickly. You save money by doing your own disjointing, because whole ducks are fresher and cheaper per pound than duck parts, and you have the added bonus of backbone, neck, and giblets for your duck stock. The only tricks are to find all the joints—thigh, leg, and wing—and to cut through cleanly at those points. You need a sharp knife, and poultry shears or a cleaver are a great help too.

1. Set the bird on its back and pull one leg away from the body. Cut through parallel to the backbone at the joint. Then cut the thigh and leg apart at the joint. Repeat with the other leg. **2.** Pull the wing away and cut through, starting inward diagonally, at the shoulder joint; then slice toward the rear. Repeat with the other wing. **3.** Using a knife or poultry shears, cut through the ribs along either side of the backbone. **4.** Open up the body and cut between the breast and the backbone. Place the breast skin-side down and push down with your hands to flatten it. **5.** Cut the breast in half lengthwise—and then into quarters if you want 10 pieces.

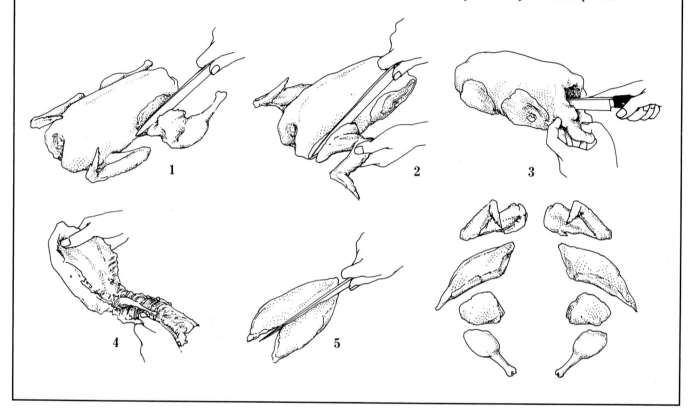

crowding, or sauté in two batches. The heat of the fat and the air spaces around the pieces facilitate browning.

Many recipes call for sautéing first, then lowering the heat and cooking the food, covered, for an additional 10 to 20 minutes. Be sure you buy a sauté pan with a tight-fitting cover. Make certain the handle is long and is comfortable to hold. Use a wooden spatula or tongs to keep food moving in the pan as you shake it over the burner. If the food sticks, a metal spatula will loosen it best. Turn the food so that all surfaces come into contact with the hot fat.

Never immerse the hot pan in cold water because this will warp the metal. Allow the pan to cool slightly, then add water and let it sit until you are ready to wash it.

The fat: Half butter and half vegetable or peanut oil is perfect for most sautéing: It heats to high temperatures without burning, yet allows a rich butter flavor. For cooking, unsalted butter tastes best and adds no extra salt.

If you prefer an all-butter flavor, clarify the butter before you begin. This means removing the milky residue, which is the part that scorches. To clarify butter, heat it in a small saucepan over medium heat and, using a cooking spoon, skim off and discard the foam as it rises to the top. Keep skimming until no more foam appears. Pour off the remaining oil—the clarified butter—leaving the milky residue at the bottom of the pan. You may clarify only the amount of butter required for the meal you are preparing, or you may make a large quantity of it and store it in your refrigerator for two to three weeks, if desired.

Some sautéing recipes in this book call for olive oil, which imparts a delicious and distinctive flavor of its own and is less sensitive than butter to high heat. Nevertheless, even the finest olive oil has some residue of fruit pulp, which will occasionally scorch. Watch carefully when you sauté in olive oil; discard any scorched oil and start with fresh, if necessary.

To sauté properly, heat the fat until it is hot but not smoking. When you see small bubbles on top of the fat, lower the heat because it is on the verge of smoking. When using butter and oil together, add butter to the hot oil. After the foam from the melting butter subsides, you are ready to sauté. If the temperature of the fat is just right, the food will sizzle when you put it in the pan.

Searing

When you sear, you brown the meat without shaking or stirring the pan. Heat the oil until it is very hot, then brown the meat over high heat for a minute or two on each side. A metal spatula is essential, for the meat will tend to stick. Wait until the meat is very brown on one side before you turn it. Vicki Cheung sears raw turkey, page 24.

Stir Frying

This technique requires very little oil, and the foods—which you stir continuously—fry quickly over very high heat. Stir frying is ideal for cooking bite-size, shredded, or thinly sliced portions of vegetables, fish, meat, or poultry, alone or in combination. Vicki Cheung stir fries rice, page 19.

Braising

Braising is simmering meats or vegetables in a relatively small amount of liquid, usually for a long period of time. Sometimes the food is browned or parboiled before braising. You may wish to flavor the braising liquid with herbs, spices, and aromatic vegetables, or use wine, stock, or tomato sauce as a medium. Leslee Reis braises turnips and onions, page 55.

Deglazing

This is an easy way to create a sauce for sautéed, braised, or roasted food. To deglaze, pour off all but 1 or 2 tablespoons of fat from the pan in which the food has been cooked. Add liquid—water, wine, or stock—and reduce the sauce over medium heat, using a wooden spoon to scrape up and blend into the sauce the concentrated juices and browned bits of food clinging to the bottom of the pan. Danièle Delpeuch uses this technique in her recipe for Turkey Paupiettes, page 70.

Blanching

Blanching, or parboiling, is an invaluable technique. Immerse vegetables for a few minutes in boiling water, then refresh them, that is, plunge them into cold water to stop their cooking and set their colors. Blanching softens or tenderizes dense or crisp vegetables, often as a preliminary to further cooking by another method, such as stir frying. Holly Garrison blanches watercress, page 61.

Steaming

Steaming is a fast and nutritious way to cook vegetables and other food. Bring water to a boil in a saucepan. Place the food in a steamer or on a rack over the liquid and cover the pan, periodically checking the water level. Keeping the food above the liquid preserves vitamins and minerals often lost in other methods of cooking. Douglas Oaks steams broccoli florets, page 42.

Broiling and Grilling

These are relatively fast ways to cook meat, poultry, and fish, giving the food a crisp exterior while leaving the inside juicy. To add flavor or moisture, brush the food with melted fat, a sauce, or a marinade before you cook.

In broiling, the food cooks directly under the heat source. In grilling, the food cooks either directly over an open fire or on a well-seasoned cast-iron or stoneware griddle placed directly over a burner.

Roasting and Baking

Roasting is a dry-heat process, usually used for large cuts of meat and poultry, that cooks the food by exposing it to heated air in an oven or, perhaps, a covered barbecue. For more even circulation of heat, the food should be placed in a shallow pan or on a rack in a pan. For greater moisture retention, baste the food with its own juices, fat, or a flavorful marinade. Holly Garrison's Menu 3 features duck skin roasted until crisp, page 63.

Baking applies to the dry-heat cooking of foods such as casseroles; small cuts of meat, fish, poultry, and vegetables; and, of course, breads and pastries. Some foods are baked tightly covered to retain their juices and flavors; others, such as breads, cakes, and cookies, are baked in open pans to release moisture.

Making Stock

Although canned stock is all right for emergencies, homemade stock has a rich flavor that is hard to match. Moreover, canned broths are likely to be oversalted.

To make your own chicken, duck, or turkey stock, save poultry parts as they accumulate and put them in a bag in the freezer; then have a rainy-day stock-making session, using the recipe below, which works equally well for any type of poultry. The skin from a yellow onion will add color; the optional veal bone will add extra flavor and richness to the stock.

3 pounds bony poultry parts, such as wings, back, and neck
1 veal knuckle (optional)
3 quarts cold water
1 yellow unpeeled onion, stuck with 2 cloves
2 stalks celery with leaves, cut in two
12 crushed peppercorns
2 carrots, scraped and cut into 2-inch lengths
4 sprigs parsley
1 bay leaf
1 tablespoon fresh thyme, or 1 teaspoon dried
Salt (optional)

1. Wash poultry parts, and veal knuckle if using, and drain. Place in large soup kettle or stockpot (any big pot) with the remaining ingredients—except salt. Cover pot and bring to a boil over medium heat.

2. Lower heat and simmer stock, partly covered, 2 to 3 hours. Skim foam and scum from top of stock several times. Add salt to taste after stock has cooked 1 hour.

3. Strain stock through fine sieve placed over large bowl. Discard solids. Let stock cool uncovered (this will speed cooling process). When completely cool, refrigerate. Fat will rise and congeal conveniently at top. You may skim it off and discard it or leave it as a protective covering.

Yield: About 10 cups

Pantry (for this volume)

A well-stocked, properly organized pantry is essential for preparing great meals in the shortest time possible. Whether your pantry consists of a small refrigerator and two or three shelves over the sink, or a large freezer, refrigerator, and entire room just off the kitchen, you must protect staples from heat and light.

In maintaining your pantry, follow these rules:

1. Store staples by kind and date. Canned goods, canisters, and spices need a separate shelf, or a separate spot on a shelf. Date all staples—shelved, refrigerated, or frozen—by writing the date directly on the package or on a bit of masking tape. Then put the oldest ones in front to be sure you use them first.

2. Store flour, sugar, and other dry ingredients in canisters or jars with tight lids. Glass and clear plastic allow you to see at a glance how much remains.

3. Keep a running grocery list so that you can note when a staple is half gone, and be sure to stock up.

ON THE SHELF:

Capers
Capers are usually packed in vinegar and less frequently in salt. If you use the latter, you should rinse them under cold water before using them.

Dried fruits
pitted prunes

Flour
all-purpose, bleached or unbleached

Garlic
Store in a cool, dry, well-ventilated place. Garlic powder and garlic salt are not adequate substitutes for fresh garlic.

Herbs and spices
The flavor of fresh herbs is much better than that of dried. Fresh herbs should be refrigerated and used as soon as possible. The following herbs are perfectly acceptable dried, but buy in small amounts, store airtight in dry area away from heat and light, and use as quickly as possible. In measuring herbs, remember that one part dried will equal three parts fresh. *Note:* Dried chives and parsley should not be on your shelf, since they have little or no flavor; frozen chives are acceptable. Buy whole spices rather than ground, as they keep their flavor much longer. Grind spices at home and store as directed for herbs.

basil

bay leaves
Cayenne pepper
cinnamon
cloves, whole and ground
coriander, whole and
    ground
cumin
curry powder
fennel seeds
mustard
nutmeg, whole and ground
oregano
paprika
    Most recipes in this book call for mild sweet imported Hungarian paprika.
pepper
    black peppercorns
    These are unripe peppercorns dried in their husks. Grind with a pepper mill for each use.
    white peppercorns
    These are the same as the black variety, but are picked ripe and husked. Use them in pale sauces when black pepper specks would spoil the appearance.
red pepper flakes (also
    called crushed red
    pepper)
saffron
    Made from the dried stigmas of a species of crocus, this spice—the most costly of all seasonings—adds both color and flavor. Use sparingly.
sage leaves
salt
    Use coarse salt—commonly available as kosher or sea—for its superior flavor, texture, and purity. Kosher

salt and sea salt are less salty than table salt. Substitute in the following proportions: three-quarters teaspoon table salt equals just under one teaspoon kosher or sea salt.
tarragon
thyme
turmeric

Honey

Hot pepper sauce

Nuts, whole, chopped, or slivered
pecans
pine nuts (pignoli)
walnuts

Oils
corn, safflower, peanut,
    or vegetable
    Because these neutral-tasting oils have high smoking points, they are good for high-heat sautéing.
olive oil
    Sample French, Greek, Spanish, and Italian oils. Olive oil ranges in color from pale yellow to dark green and in taste from mild and delicate to rich and fruity. Different olive oils can be used for different purposes: for example, stronger ones for cooking, lighter ones for salads. The finest quality olive oil is labeled extra-virgin or virgin.
sesame oil
    Dark amber-colored Oriental-style oil, used for seasoning; do not substitute light cold-pressed sesame oil.

Onions
Store all dry-skinned onions in a cool, dry, well-ventilated place.
red or Italian onions
    Zesty tasting and generally eaten raw. The perfect salad onion.
shallots
    The most subtle member of the onion family, the shallot has a delicate garlic flavor.
yellow onions
    All-purpose cooking onions, strong in taste.

Potatoes, boiling and baking
"New" potatoes are not a particular kind of potato, but any potato that has not been stored.

Rice
long-grain white rice
    Slender grains, much longer than they are wide, that become light and fluffy when cooked and are best for general use.

Soy Sauce
Chinese
    Usually salty and richly flavored—for cooking.

Stock, chicken and beef
For maximum flavor and quality, your own stock is best (see recipe page 11), but canned stock, or broth, is adequate for most recipes and convenient to have on hand.

Sugar
granulated sugar

Tomatoes
Italian plum tomatoes
    Canned plum tomatoes

(preferably imported) are an acceptable substitute for fresh.

tomato paste

Sometimes available in tubes, which can be refrigerated and kept for future use after a small amount is gone. With canned paste, spoon out unused portions in one-tablespoon amounts onto waxed paper and freeze, then lift the frozen paste off and store in a plastic container.

Vinegars

distilled white vinegar
red and white wine
       vinegars
tarragon vinegar

A white wine vinegar flavored with fresh tarragon, it is especially good in salads.

Wines and spirits

brandy
Madeira
ruby port
sherry, dry
white wine, dry

Worcestershire sauce

IN THE REFRIGERATOR:

Basil

Though fresh basil is widely available only in summer, try to use it whenever possible to replace dried; the flavor is markedly superior. Stand the stems, preferably with roots intact, in a jar of water, and loosely cover leaves with a plastic bag.

Bread crumbs

You need never buy bread crumbs. To make fresh crumbs, use fresh or day-old bread and process in food processor or blender. For dried, toast bread 30 minutes in preheated 250-degree oven, turning occasionally to prevent slices from browning. Proceed as for fresh. Store bread crumbs in an airtight container: fresh crumbs in the refrigerator, and dried crumbs in a cool, dry place. Either type may also be frozen for several weeks

if tightly wrapped in a plastic bag.

Butter

Many cooks prefer unsalted butter because of its finer flavor and because it does not burn as easily as salted.

Cheese

Cheddar cheese, sharp

A firm cheese, ranging in color from nearly white to yellow. Cheddar is a versatile cooking cheese.

Gruyère

This firm cheese resembles Swiss, but has smaller holes and a sharper flavor. A quality Gruyère will have a slight "gleam" in its eyes, or holes.

Parmesan cheese

Avoid the pre-grated packaged variety; it is very expensive and almost flavorless. Buy Parmesan by the quarter- or half-pound wedge and grate as needed: 4 ounces produces about one cup of grated cheese.

Chives

Refrigerate fresh chives wrapped in plastic. You may also buy small pots of growing chives—keep them on a windowsill and snip as needed.

Coriander

Also called *cilantro* or Chinese parsley, its pungent leaves resemble flat-leaf parsley. Keep in a glass of water covered with a plastic bag.

Cream

half-and-half
heavy cream
light cream
sour cream

Eggs

Will keep 4 to 5 weeks in refrigerator. For best results, bring to room temperature before using, except when separating.

Ginger, fresh

Found in the produce section. Wrap in a paper towel, then in plastic, and refrigerate; it will keep for about 1 month, but should be checked weekly for mold. Or, if you prefer, store it in

the freezer, where it will last about 3 months. Firm, smooth-skinned ginger need not be peeled.

Lemons

In addition to its many uses in cooking, a slice of lemon rubbed over cut apples and pears will keep them from discoloring. Do not substitute bottled juice or lemon extract.

Limes
Milk
Mustards

The recipes in this book usually call for Dijon or coarse-grained mustard.

Parsley

The two most commonly available kinds of parsley are flat-leaf and curly; they can be used interchangeably when necessary. Flat-leaf parsley has a more distinctive flavor and is generally preferred in cooking. Curly parsley wilts less easily and is excellent for garnishing. Store parsley in a glass of water and cover loosely with a plastic bag. It will keep for a week in the refrigerator. Or wash and dry it, and refrigerate in a small plastic bag with a dry paper towel inside to absorb any moisture.

Scallions

Scallions have a mild onion flavor. Store wrapped in plastic.

Yogurt

Equipment

Proper cooking equipment makes the work light and is a good cook's most prized possession. You can cook expertly without a store-bought steamer or even a food processor, but basic pans, knives, and a few other items are indispensable. Below are the things you need—and some attractive options—for preparing the menus in this volume.

Pots and pans
Large kettle or stockpot
3 skillets (large, medium, small) with covers; one with oven-proof handle
2 heavy-gauge sauté pans, 10 to 12 inches in diameter, with covers
3 saucepans with covers (1-, 2-, and 4-quart capacities)
> Choose heavy-gauge enameled cast-iron, plain cast-iron, aluminum-clad stainless steel, or aluminum (but you need at least one saucepan that is not aluminum). Best—but very expensive—is tin-lined copper.

Nonaluminum double boiler
14- to 16-inch wok
Large flameproof casserole or Dutch oven with cover
Roasting pan with rack
2 shallow baking pans (13 x 9 x 2-inch, and 8 x 8-inch)
2 cookie sheets (17 x 11-inch and 15 x 10-inch)
9-inch pie pan
Large ovenproof baking dish
Ovenproof serving platters
Ovenproof serving bowl
Salad bowl

Knives
> A carbon-steel knife takes a sharp edge but tends to rust. You must wash and dry it after each use; otherwise it can blacken foods and counter tops. Good-quality stainless-steel knives, frequently honed, are less trouble and will serve just as well in the home kitchen. Never put a fine knife in the dishwasher. Rinse it, dry it, and put it away—but not loose in a drawer. Knives will stay sharp if they have their own storage rack.

Small paring knife
10-inch chef's knife
Boning knife
Sharpening steel

Other cooking tools
2 sets of mixing bowls in graduated sizes, one set preferably glass or stainless steel
Colander with a round base (stainless steel, aluminum, or enamel)
2 sieves in fine and coarse mesh
2 strainers in fine and coarse mesh
2 sets of measuring cups and spoons in graduated sizes
> One for dry ingredients, another for shortenings and liquids.

2 cooking spoons
Slotted spoon
Long-handled wooden spoons
2 metal spatulas or turners (for lifting hot foods from pans)
Fork (for combining dry ingredients)
Rubber or vinyl spatula (for folding in ingredients)
Rolling pin or kitchen mallet
Grater (metal, with several sizes of holes)
> A rotary grater is handy for hard cheese.

Small wire whisk
Pair of metal tongs
Wooden board
Garlic press
Vegetable peeler
Mortar and pestle
Pastry brush for basting (a small, new paintbrush that is not nylon serves well)
Cooling rack
Kitchen shears
Kitchen timer
Cheesecloth
Aluminum foil
Paper towels
Plastic wrap
Waxed paper
Kitchen string
Oven mitts or potholders

Electric appliances
Food processor or blender
> A blender will do most of the work required in this volume, but a food processor will do it more quickly and in larger volume. A food processor should be considered a necessity, not a luxury, for anyone who enjoys cooking.

Electric mixer

Optional cooking tools
Salad spinner
Butter warmer
Melon baller
Spice grinder
Apple corer
Salad servers
Citrus juicer
> Inexpensive glass kind from the dime store will do.

Nutmeg grater
Zester
Metal skewer
Roll of masking tape or white paper tape for labeling and dating

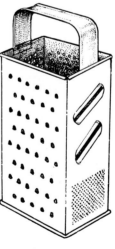

GRATER

COLANDER

STRAINER

FOOD
PROCESSOR

RUBBER
SPATULA

WHISK

MIXING BOWLS

METAL
SPATULA

VEGETABLE PEELER

SHARPENING STEEL

CHEF'S KNIFE

DOUBLE
BOILER

PARING KNIFE

CASSEROLE

SAUCEPANS

SAUTÉ PAN

SKILLET

Vicki Cheung

W hen confronted with a culinary problem such as how to prepare turkey or duck in an hour, Vicki Cheung usually considers how a classically trained Chinese cook would solve it. For this volume she came up with a quick way to cook a duck Chinese-style (it normally takes several hours or even days) and tailored two Asian recipes to suit turkey, a bird rarely eaten in China or India.

To prepare the duck in Menu 1, she adapts a Cantonese cooking technique called *ch'a-shao,* or fork roasting, in which the meat is suspended over water while cooking. Here the duck is split, then stretched flat on a roasting rack over water. With its maximum surface exposed, the duck roasts rapidly in the hot oven and bastes in its own fat. With the duck she serves a classic northern Chinese stir-fried rice, which can be made with leftover rice to save time.

Menu 2 focuses on the flavors of India and features marinated, oven-baked turkey strips as the entrée. The seasonings in the two marinades are like those used in Indian *tandoori* (clay oven) cooking. The turkey's spicy flavors are countered by braised stuffed cucumbers.

Menu 3 is influenced by Chinese, Indian, Malaysian, and European cooking. The turkey curry contains lemon grass, coconut cream, shredded coconut, fresh coriander, curry powder, ginger, and chilies. The accompanying green beans are tossed with a piquant sesame-soy vinaigrette.

For a dramatic presentation, serve the whole crisp-skinned butterflied duck on a large platter with fresh coriander, and carve it afterward. Offer a bowl of savory fried rice as a side dish and duck sauce if you like.

Fragrant Duck
Savory Fried Rice

The cook suggests an alternative method for preparing the duck in advance, beginning 24 hours or more before cooking. Omit step 1 of the recipe and follow steps 2 through 7. Let the duck rest for 30 minutes. Skip step 8 and mix the glaze (step 9), substituting a light, colorless corn syrup for the honey; then brush the glaze over the skin. Place the duck, skin-side up, on a rack in a roasting pan, and leave it in a *cool*, drafty place (or in front of a fan) for at least 24 hours. This allows the marinade to penetrate, and the drying process helps crisp the skin during roasting. When ready to cook, roast the duck for 35 minutes at 425 degrees, then follow steps 10 through 15 of the recipe.

You can purchase five-spice powder in the Oriental section of many supermarkets. The mixture includes cloves, cinnamon, Szechwan peppercorns, fennel, and star anise.

WHAT TO DRINK

Tea is the traditional beverage with Chinese meals. The cook recommends either a light and fragrant jasmine flavor or a stronger black tea. If you prefer wine, try a fruity red with good body, such as a young Chianti.

SHOPPING LIST AND STAPLES

4- to 4½-pound whole duck
4 thick slices bacon (about ¼ pound)
Small bunch celery
Small bunch scallions
1 bunch coriander
2 cloves garlic
2 large eggs
6 tablespoons vegetable oil, approximately
2 teaspoons sesame oil
¼ cup white or cider vinegar
2 teaspoons light soy sauce
15-ounce jar hoisin sauce
7-ounce jar duck sauce (optional)
2 tablespoons honey
1 cup long-grain rice
2-ounce jar five-spice powder
Salt and freshly ground black pepper

UTENSILS

Wok or large heavy-gauge skillet
Medium-size heavy-gauge sauté pan with cover
Medium-size saucepan
Small saucepan
17 x 11-inch roasting pan with rack
13 x 9-inch jelly-roll pan
3 small bowls
Measuring cups and spoons
Chef's knife
Paring knife
2 wooden spoons or wok spatulas
Slotted spoon
Bulb baster or large metal spoon
Metal skewer
Pastry brush

START-TO-FINISH STEPS

1. Follow duck recipe steps 1 through 6.
2. Follow rice recipe steps 1 through 3 and duck recipe steps 7 and 8.
3. Follow rice recipe steps 4 through 9.
4. Follow duck recipe steps 9 through 14.
5. While duck is resting, follow rice recipe steps 10 through 13.
6. Follow duck recipe step 15 and serve with rice.

RECIPES

Fragrant Duck

1 tablespoon salt
½ teaspoon freshly ground black pepper
½ teaspoon five-spice powder
2 cloves garlic
3 tablespoons hoisin sauce
4- to 4½-pound whole duck
2 tablespoons honey
¼ cup white or cider vinegar
1 bunch coriander
7-ounce jar duck sauce (optional)

1. Preheat oven to 425 degrees.
2. Bring 2 quarts of water to a boil in medium-size saucepan over high heat.
3. Combine salt, pepper, and five-spice powder in small bowl and set aside.
4. Peel and mince enough garlic to measure 1 tablespoon. Combine garlic and hoisin sauce in another small bowl, stir to combine, and set aside.
5. Remove excess fat from cavity of duck and trim off neck

skin, discarding both. Break off wings at first joint and place duck, breast-side up, on cutting surface. With sharp chef's knife, split duck lengthwise by cutting through wishbone, breast meat, and keel bone. Trim off tail and discard. Using hands, press breast sides down to flatten duck. Rinse duck under cold running water and place, skin-side up, in roasting pan.

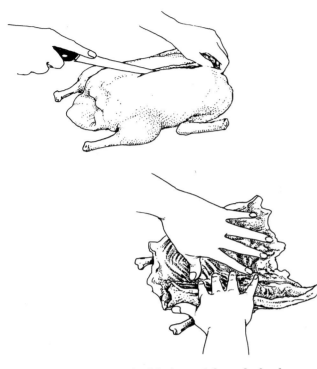

6. Place roasting pan in kitchen sink and slowly pour 2 quarts boiling water over duck. Let duck soak in hot bath 5 minutes.

7. Remove duck from pan and pour off water; dry duck and pan with paper towels. Rub *both* sides of duck with salt and spice mixture, and brush *bone* side only with hoisin mixture.

8. Line roasting pan with foil and fit with rack. Place duck, skin-side up, on rack, add 1 cup hot water to pan, and roast in oven 35 minutes.

9. Combine honey and vinegar in small saucepan and warm over medium heat until honey dissolves, about 2 minutes.

10. Using bulb baster or large spoon, drain off oily fat from roasting pan and raise oven temperature to 475 degrees. Brush duck skin with honey glaze and roast another 15 minutes.

11. Wash coriander and dry with paper towels; trim stems and discard.

12. If using duck sauce, pour into small serving bowl.

13. Test duck for doneness by inserting a metal skewer into the leg and breast. If juices run clear, remove duck from oven. If juices are still red, return duck to oven and roast another few minutes.

14. Transfer duck to serving platter and allow to rest at least 10 minutes before serving.

15. Surround duck with coriander leaves and serve with duck sauce, if desired.

Savory Fried Rice

4 thick slices bacon (about ¼ pound)
1 cup long-grain rice
3 stalks celery, approximately
Small bunch scallions
6 tablespoons vegetable oil, approximately
2 large eggs
Salt
2 teaspoons light soy sauce
2 teaspoons sesame oil

1. Bring 2 cups cold water to a boil in a medium-size heavy-gauge sauté pan over high heat.

2. While water is heating, cut bacon into ¼-inch pieces and set aside.

3. Add rice to boiling water, stir, and return to a boil. Reduce heat, cover pan, and simmer rice gently, without stirring, about 20 minutes, or until liquid is completely absorbed.

4. Wash celery and scallions, and dry with paper towels. Trim off ends and discard. Cut enough celery crosswise into ¼-inch-thick pieces to measure 1 cup; chop enough scallions to measure ¼ cup.

5. Heat 1 tablespoon vegetable oil in wok or large skillet over high heat. While oil is heating, combine eggs, a pinch of salt, and 1 tablespoon cold water in small bowl and beat with fork until blended. Add egg mixture to hot skillet and scramble with wooden spoon or wok spatula, stirring to separate curds. When eggs are cooked, turn out onto plate and set aside. Rinse out bowl.

6. Return wok or skillet to medium heat. Add bacon and fry, stirring occasionally, 3 to 4 minutes, or until crisp.

7. Meanwhile, line jelly-roll pan with foil.

8. With slotted spoon, transfer bacon to paper towels to drain. Pour off bacon fat from pan and reserve; wipe out pan.

9. With fork, fluff rice and turn into foil-lined pan. Place rice in freezer to cool at least 10 minutes.

10. In the small bowl, combine 1 tablespoon salt and ¼ cup water, and stir until salt is dissolved.

11. Heat wok or skillet over high heat until a bead of water evaporates on contact. Add enough vegetable oil and bacon fat, or just bacon fat, to measure 4 to 5 tablespoons. When oil is hot, add rice to pan and stir fry, using 2 wooden spoons or wok spatulas, 2 to 3 minutes.

12. Add soy sauce and stir to combine with rice. One teaspoon at a time, add salted water to taste, tossing between each addition.

13. Add bacon, celery, and eggs, and toss briskly until combined and heated through. Add sesame oil to rice mixture, sprinkle with scallions, and toss again. Turn rice into serving bowl.

LEFTOVER SUGGESTION

Reserve the wings, neck, and giblets, as well as the carcass, to make a rich, flavorful duck stock (see page 11) for soups and sauces.

Tandoori-style Turkey
Braised Stuffed Cucumbers

Tart tandoori-*style turkey bakes until golden and is then garnished with lemon, onion rings, and parsley. Braised cucumbers with a fennel-seasoned stuffing help cool the palate, as does the optional sweet chutney.*

The authentic Indian *tandoor* oven is a deep clay-lined pit with the cooking fuel at the bottom, which simultaneously grills, bakes, and roasts food. *Tandoor*-cooked meat is especially tender and moist. Before cooking, the meat is soaked in a spicy yogurt-based marinade that contains betel nuts or crushed papaya as a tenderizer, and cochineal, a natural dye that gives the meat its orange color.

For this recipe, the cook tenderizes the turkey strips by first pounding them, then soaking them in a mixture of two marinades—one containing lemon juice and vinegar and the other yogurt. To give the meat its characteristic tint, she suggests an optional red food coloring. The turkey is baked in a very hot oven until the marinade forms a crust; alternatively, you can cook the turkey over hot coals on an open grill.

WHAT TO DRINK

An India Pale ale or a slightly sweet German Riesling would be refreshing with this meal. The cook also recommends "shandy"—a mixture of beer, lemonade, and a spritz of sparkling water.

SHOPPING LIST AND STAPLES

1- to 1½-pound section of boneless turkey breast
¾ pound mushrooms
2 cucumbers (about 1½ pounds total weight)
Medium-size onion, plus 1 onion for garnish (optional)
Small red bell pepper
Small bunch parsley
5 cloves garlic
2-inch-long piece fresh ginger
1 lemon, plus 1 additional lemon for garnish (optional)
1 cup chicken stock, preferably homemade (see page 11), or canned
3 tablespoons unsalted butter (optional)
½ pint plain yogurt
2 tablespoons vegetable oil, plus 2 tablespoons (if not using butter)
2 tablespoons white vinegar
12½-ounce jar mango chutney (optional)
½ cup dry bread crumbs, preferably flavored
2 teaspoons ground coriander
2 teaspoons ground cumin
1 teaspoon ground turmeric

1 teaspoon dry mustard
1 teaspoon paprika
½ teaspoon mild curry powder
½ teaspoon fennel seeds
¼ teaspoon ground cinnamon
¼ teaspoon ground nutmeg
¼ teaspoon ground mace
½ teaspoon Cayenne pepper
1 teaspoon red food coloring, approximately (optional)
Salt
Freshly ground black pepper

UTENSILS

Food processor or blender
Medium-size skillet or Dutch oven with cover
Small heavy-gauge saucepan (if using clarified butter)
13 x 9-inch roasting pan with rack
17 x 11-inch cookie sheet (if using electric range)
Large bowl
Small bowl
Measuring cups and spoons
Chef's knife
Paring knife
2 wooden spoons
Metal tongs
Vegetable peeler
Melon baller (optional)
Scissors
Meat pounder or rolling pin
Kitchen string

START-TO-FINISH STEPS

Fifteen minutes ahead: Clarify butter (see page 10), if using, for cucumbers.

1. Rinse parsley and dry with paper towels. Reserve 4 sprigs for garnish for turkey recipe, if desired, and chop enough to measure 1 tablespoon for cucumbers recipe.
2. Follow turkey recipe steps 1 through 7.
3. Follow cucumbers recipe steps 1 through 3.
4. Follow turkey recipe step 8.
5. Follow cucumbers recipe steps 4 through 7.
6. While cucumbers are simmering, follow turkey recipe steps 9 through 11.
7. Follow cucumbers recipe step 8, turkey recipe step 12, and serve.

RECIPES

Tandoori-style Turkey

First marinade:
1 lemon
2 tablespoons white vinegar
1 teaspoon salt
1 teaspoon paprika
5 drops red food coloring (optional)

Second marinade:
Medium-size onion
4 cloves garlic
2-inch-long piece fresh ginger
Small red bell pepper
2 tablespoons vegetable oil
2 teaspoons ground coriander
2 teaspoons ground cumin
1 teaspoon freshly ground black pepper
1 teaspoon ground turmeric
1 teaspoon dry mustard
½ teaspoon mild curry powder
1 teaspoon salt
¼ teaspoon ground cinnamon
¼ teaspoon ground nutmeg
¼ teaspoon ground mace
½ teaspoon Cayenne pepper
½ pint plain yogurt
½ teaspoon red food coloring (optional)

1- to 1½-pound section of boneless turkey breast

Garnishes (optional):
1 lemon
1 onion
4 sprigs parsley

12½-ounce jar mango chutney (optional)

1. For first marinade: Juice lemon. Combine lemon juice, vinegar, salt, paprika, and 5 drops food coloring, if using, in small bowl.
2. For second marinade: Peel and finely chop onion, garlic, and ginger. Halve, core, seed, and chop bell pepper.
3. In food processor or blender, combine onion, garlic, ginger, pepper, oil, and remaining dry ingredients, and process until blended. Add yogurt, and ½ teaspoon red food coloring, if using, and blend until liquefied.
4. Remove skin and any excess fat from turkey breast. Place meat on flat surface and cut horizontally into 2 flat pieces about 1½ inches thick. Following the contours of the breast, cut turkey into 1½ x 1½ x 6-inch strips. Each half-breast of turkey should yield 6 or 7 strips.

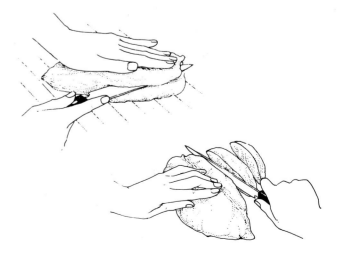

21

5. Place 2 or 3 strips about 2 inches apart between two sheets of waxed paper and flatten with meat pounder or rolling pin to about ½ inch thick. Repeat with remaining strips.

6. In large bowl, combine flattened turkey strips and first marinade, and marinate 10 minutes.

7. Preheat oven to 500 degrees.

8. Add second marinade to first and stir to combine; marinate turkey another 10 minutes.

9. Line roasting pan with foil and fit with rack. Place turkey pieces on rack and bake in middle of oven 15 to 20 minutes, or until the marinade is slightly dry and baked on. (If heating element is inside oven, shield it by placing cookie sheet on highest oven rack; then place turkey below.)

10. Rinse lemon for garnish, if using, and dry. Halve lemon and cut each half into 4 wedges.

11. Peel onion for garnish, if using, and cut into ¼-inch-thick slices; separate into rings.

12. Divide turkey among 4 dinner plates. Garnish each serving with lemon wedges, onion rings, and a sprig of parsley, and serve with mango chutney on the side, if desired.

Braised Stuffed Cucumbers

2 cucumbers (about 1½ pounds total weight)
Salt
¾ pound mushrooms
1 clove garlic
1 tablespoon chopped parsley
2 tablespoons clarified butter (see page 10) or vegetable oil
½ teaspoon fennel seeds
½ cup dry bread crumbs, preferably flavored
Freshly ground black pepper
1 cup chicken stock

1. Peel cucumbers and score with fork. Halve each cucumber lengthwise; scoop out seeds with melon baller or teaspoon and discard. Rub each cucumber half with ½ teaspoon salt and set aside.

2. Wipe mushrooms clean with damp paper towels. Peel garlic.

3. Combine garlic, mushrooms, and parsley in food processor, if using, and chop coarsely. Or, chop with chef's knife.

4. Heat clarified butter or vegetable oil in medium-size skillet or Dutch oven over medium-high heat. Add mushroom mixture and fennel seeds, and sauté, stirring, 1 to 2 minutes, or until mushrooms are soft.

5. Stir in bread crumbs, add salt and pepper to taste, and remove skillet from heat.

6. Rinse cucumber halves under cold running water and dry with paper towels. Fill each of the cavities with mushroom mixture and reassemble cucumbers by placing halves together. Tie each cucumber securely with kitchen string.

7. Rinse skillet, add stock, and bring to a boil over high heat. Add cucumbers, bring stock to a simmer, cover, and cook 15 to 20 minutes, or until cucumbers are tender when tested with a fork.

8. Transfer cucumbers to cutting surface. Remove strings and discard. Cut each cucumber crosswise into 6 slices and divide among dinner plates.

ADDED TOUCH

Pilau, or pilaf, is a well-seasoned rice dish frequently eaten in India and the Middle East. To augment it for a luncheon main course, add diced pieces of meat, poultry, or cooked vegetables.

Rice Pilau

¼ cup pine nuts
Medium-size onion
2 tablespoons clarified butter (see page 10) or vegetable oil
1 cup long-grain rice
2 cups chicken or turkey stock
½ to 1 teaspoon saffron threads
¼ cup raisins
¼ cup frozen peas
2 bay leaves
4 whole cloves
Pinch of nutmeg
Salt

1. Preheat oven to 350 degrees.

2. Place pine nuts in pie plate and toast in oven, shaking plate occasionally to prevent scorching, 8 to 10 minutes, or until golden.

3. Meanwhile, peel and coarsely chop enough onion to measure ½ cup.

4. Heat butter or oil in medium-size heavy-gauge saucepan over medium-high heat. Add chopped onion, reduce heat to medium, and sauté, stirring occasionally, 4 to 5 minutes, or until golden.

5. With slotted spoon, transfer onions to plate; set aside.

6. Remove pine nuts from oven and set aside to cool.

7. Add rice to pan and sauté over medium heat, stirring occasionally, 7 to 8 minutes, or until rice is translucent.

8. Stir in stock, and saffron to taste, and bring stock to a boil.

9. Stir in pine nuts, onions, raisins, peas, bay leaves, cloves, nutmeg, and salt to taste. Cover, reduce heat, and simmer, without stirring, 20 minutes, or until all liquid is absorbed.

10. Remove pan from heat and allow to rest 5 to 10 minutes.

11. Fluff rice with fork. Remove bay leaves and cloves, and discard. Serve rice hot.

LEFTOVER SUGGESTION

Leftover *tandoori*-style turkey can be ground up for use in croquettes, or cut into small chunks to add to fried rice or a tossed green salad.

Malaysian Turkey-Vegetable Curry
Sesame Green Beans

Individual bowls of curried turkey and vegetables are served with sesame green beans and bowls of raisins, nuts, and coconut.

Unsweetened coconut cream blended with curry powder and other seasonings makes the sauce for this turkey dish. You can buy canned coconut cream in Oriental and Middle Eastern groceries and in many supermarkets, or easily make it at home. Place two cups of packaged unsweetened shredded coconut in the container of a blender or food processor and add 2½ cups of boiling water. Cover and blend 30 seconds, then strain through a fine sieve into a large bowl, pressing out all of the moisture. This should yield about 2 cups of coconut cream.

WHAT TO DRINK

A cold lager or a well-chilled white wine with plenty of flavor, such as a California Sauvignon Blanc, would be good with these dishes.

SHOPPING LIST AND STAPLES

2 to 2½ pounds boneless turkey breast
1 pound green beans
2 medium-size all-purpose potatoes (about ½ pound total weight)
2 carrots (about ½ pound total weight)
2 medium-size onions (about 1 pound total weight)
2 fresh hot red chilies (optional)
2-inch-long piece fresh ginger
4 cloves garlic
Large bunch coriander
15-ounce can unsweetened coconut cream
6 tablespoons unsalted butter, approximately, or 5 tablespoons vegetable oil
1 teaspoon sesame oil
¼ cup tarragon or other flavored vinegar
2 tablespoons dark soy sauce or tamari
1 cup all-purpose flour
2 tablespoons sugar
6-ounce package shredded unsweetened coconut
15-ounce package golden raisins (optional)
4-ounce can blanched slivered almonds (optional)
2½-ounce jar sesame seeds
3 tablespoons curry powder

23

2 bay leaves
1 blade lemon grass (optional)
Salt
Freshly ground black pepper

UTENSILS

Food processor (optional)
Blender
Stockpot or large saucepan
Dutch oven
Small heavy-gauge skillet
9-inch pie pan
Large bowl
2 medium-size bowls
Small bowl
Colander
Measuring cups and spoons
Chef's knife
Paring knife
2 wooden spoons
Slotted spoon
Rubber spatula
Vegetable peeler
Rubber gloves (if using chilies)

START-TO-FINISH STEPS

Fifteen minutes ahead: Clarify butter (see page 10), if using, for turkey recipe.

1. Follow turkey recipe steps 1 through 14.
2. Follow green beans recipe steps 1 through 5 and turkey recipe step 15, if using almonds.
3. Follow green beans recipe steps 6 through 9.
4. Follow turkey recipe step 16 and serve with green beans.

RECIPES

Malaysian Turkey-Vegetable Curry

½ cup shredded unsweetened coconut, plus 1 cup as condiment (optional)
2 medium-size onions (about 1 pound total weight)
4 cloves garlic
2-inch-long piece fresh ginger
Large bunch coriander
2 fresh hot red chilies (optional)
5 tablespoons clarified butter (see page 10) or vegetable oil
3 tablespoons curry powder
2 teaspoons salt
2 teaspoons freshly ground black pepper
2 cups unsweetened coconut cream, approximately
1 tablespoon sugar
2 medium-size all-purpose potatoes (about ½ pound total weight)
2 carrots (about ½ pound total weight)

1 blade lemon grass (optional)
2 to 2½ pounds boneless turkey breast
1 cup all-purpose flour
2 bay leaves
½ cup blanched slivered almonds (optional)
1 cup golden raisins (optional)

1. In small heavy-gauge skillet, toast ½ cup shredded coconut over medium heat, stirring continuously, 4 to 5 minutes, or until fragrant. Transfer immediately to blender. Wipe out skillet.
2. Peel onions, garlic, and ginger and coarsely chop in food processor fitted with steel blade or with chef's knife.
3. Rinse and dry coriander; trim off stems. Chop enough to measure ¾ cup and set aside. Wearing rubber gloves, wash chilies, if using, and dry with paper towels. Trim off stems and cut into ⅛-inch-thick rings.
4. Heat 2 tablespoons clarified butter or oil in Dutch oven over medium-high heat. Add onion mixture and sauté, stirring occasionally, 4 minutes, or until onions are golden brown.
5. Stir in ½ cup coriander, curry powder, 1 teaspoon salt, and 1 teaspoon pepper. Add chilies (including seeds for a much hotter flavor), if desired, and stir to combine. Reduce heat to low and cook mixture, stirring occasionally, 2 to 3 minutes.
6. Transfer mixture to blender, add coconut cream and sugar, and blend at high speed until liquefied. Set curry mixture aside in blender container. Wipe Dutch oven clean.
7. Fill medium-size bowl half full with cold water. Peel potatoes, cut each into 8 pieces, and place in cold water. Trim and peel carrots; cut into ¼-inch-thick slices and set aside. If using lemon grass, cut into 1-inch-long pieces.
8. Preheat oven to 350 degrees.
9. Remove skin from turkey, if necessary, and discard. Cut meat into 1- to 1½-inch cubes.
10. Combine flour, remaining teaspoon salt, and 1 teaspoon pepper in plastic food storage bag; shake to combine. Add about 1 cup cubed turkey to flour mixture and shake until evenly coated. Remove turkey from bag, shake off excess flour, and transfer to platter. Repeat for remaining turkey.
11. Heat remaining 3 tablespoons clarified butter or oil in Dutch oven over medium-high heat. Add enough turkey cubes to cover bottom without crowding and sear, tossing with 2 wooden spoons, about 8 minutes, or until evenly browned. With slotted spoon, transfer seared turkey to large plate and repeat with remaining turkey. When last batch of turkey is browned, return all turkey to Dutch oven.
12. Stir in onion-curry mixture. Add 1 to 2 cups of water to blender, depending on desired thickness of sauce, shake container gently to dissolve remaining residue, and add to Dutch oven. Add bay leaves, and lemon grass if using, and bring to a simmer, stirring, over medium-high heat.
13. Drain potatoes. Reduce heat under turkey to low, add potatoes and carrots, and cook, uncovered, stirring occa-

sionally, 20 to 30 minutes, or until potatoes are fork-tender.

14. If using almonds, place in pie pan and toast in oven, shaking pan occasionally to prevent scorching, 7 minutes, or until golden.

15. Remove almonds from oven and set aside to cool.

16. Remove bay leaves and lemon grass from turkey and discard. Divide turkey and vegetables among 4 serving bowls or plates, sprinkle each serving with remaining coriander, and serve with golden raisins, 1 cup shredded coconut, and toasted almonds, if desired.

Sesame Green Beans

Salt
1 pound green beans
1 teaspoon sesame oil
¼ cup tarragon or other flavored vinegar
2 tablespoons dark soy sauce or tamari
1 tablespoon sugar
1 tablespoon sesame seeds

1. In stockpot or large saucepan, bring 3 quarts of water and 1 teaspoon salt to a boil over high heat.

2. Meanwhile, trim off ends of beans. Place beans in colander and rinse under cold running water.

3. Add beans to boiling water and cook about 3 minutes after water returns to a boil, or until beans are crisp-tender.

4. Meanwhile, place 6 to 8 ice cubes in medium-size bowl and fill half full with cold water.

5. Turn beans into colander and drain. Plunge beans into ice water and then return to colander and drain again.

6. Combine oil, vinegar, soy sauce, sugar, and ¼ teaspoon salt in large bowl and beat with fork until sugar dissolves.

7. Dry beans with paper towels, add to dressing, and toss until well coated. Cover bowl and refrigerate until ready to serve.

8. In small dry heavy-gauge skillet, toast sesame seeds over medium heat, shaking pan to prevent scorching, 2 to 3 minutes, or until fragrant. Transfer seeds to small bowl; set aside.

9. Drain dressing from beans, sprinkle beans with sesame seeds, and toss to combine. Divide beans among dinner plates.

ADDED TOUCH

Satay (Southeast Asia's version of kebab) consists of bite-sized bits of meat or fish that are threaded onto a bamboo skewer then grilled. Serve *satay* as an appetizer or with a salad for a light lunch or dinner. Here it is dipped into a sweet and spicy peanut-coconut sauce. Thin any leftover sauce with coconut cream and use it as a salad dressing.

Shrimp Satay

1 pound large shrimp (about 16 to 20)

Marinade:
Small bunch fresh coriander

Large lime
1-inch-long piece fresh ginger
½ teaspoon salt
1 tablespoon sugar

Garnishes:
1 head Bibb lettuce
Medium-size tomato or 8 cherry tomatoes
Medium-size onion
Cucumber

Peanut-Coconut Dip:
½ cup unsweetened coconut cream
½ cup smooth or crunchy peanut butter
1 tablespoon hoisin sauce
2 teaspoons Oriental fish sauce or light soy sauce
1 teaspoon dark soy sauce
¼ to ½ teaspoon Cayenne pepper (optional)

1. Soak 4 bamboo skewers in cold water for about 15 minutes to prevent scorching.

2. Pinch off legs of shrimp, several at a time, then bend back and snap off sharp, beaklike piece of shell just above tail. Remove shell and discard. Using sharp paring knife, make shallow incision along back of each shrimp, exposing black digestive vein. Extract vein and discard. Rinse shrimp under cold running water; dry with paper towels.

3. Wash coriander and dry with paper towels. Trim off stems and discard; chop enough leaves to measure 2 tablespoons. Rinse lime and dry with paper towel. Grate enough lime rind to measure ½ teaspoon; squeeze enough juice to measure 2 tablespoons. Peel ginger and grate enough to measure 1 teaspoon.

4. In medium-size bowl, combine lime juice and rind, ginger, coriander, salt, and sugar, and stir to combine. Add shrimp and toss until well coated.

5. To prepare garnishes: Wash lettuce and dry in salad spinner or with paper towels. Remove any bruised or discolored leaves and discard; reserve remaining leaves. Wash tomato and dry. Core and halve tomato; cut each half into quarters. Peel onion and cut into ¼-inch-thick slices; separate into rings. Peel cucumber, halve lengthwise, and remove seeds with melon baller or teaspoon. Halve again lengthwise and cut crosswise into 1-inch-long pieces.

6. Line broiler pan with foil. Preheat broiler.

7. Combine all dip ingredients in food processor or blender and blend until smooth. Divide among 4 ramekins or small custard cups; set aside.

8. Curl shrimp into crescent shape and thread bamboo skewer through tail section and head section. Repeat with remaining shrimp, threading 4 to 5 per skewer.

9. Place skewered shrimp on broiler rack in pan and broil 4 to 5 inches away from heat about 3 minutes per side, or until shrimp are opaque.

10. While shrimps are broiling, divide lettuce leaves among 4 plates. Top with 2 tomato wedges or 2 cherry tomatoes and scatter cucumbers and onion rings over lettuce.

11. Transfer skewers to dinner plates and serve with peanut-coconut dip.

Stuffed Paillard of Turkey
Stir-Fried Broccoli with Red Bell Pepper and Lemon

To provide contrasting piquancy to the *paillard* of turkey, serve an assortment of mustards such as a dark and spicy German Düsseldorf, an herb-flavored Dijon, or a coarsely ground Creole. Or try a highly seasoned fruit chutney or *mostarda di Cremona* (candied fruits in a mustard syrup imported from Cremona, Italy). This menu does not need a starch, but a crusty French bread served warm would be a good addition.

WHAT TO DRINK

A full-bodied white wine, such as a reasonably priced French Chardonnay, Mâcon, Mercurey, or Saint-Véran, would stand up to these dishes.

SHOPPING LIST AND STAPLES

2½-pound turkey breast, skinned and boned (about 1½ pounds meat, in one piece)
1 pound ground turkey
¼ pound baked ham, unsliced
2 large bunches broccoli (about 2½ pounds total weight)
Medium-size red bell pepper
Small bunch watercress for garnish (optional)
Large clove garlic
Small bunch fresh chives, or 2-ounce package frozen
Small bunch fresh sage, or 1 teaspoon dried
1 lemon
2 eggs
1 teaspoon cream or milk
4 tablespoons unsalted butter, approximately
2 tablespoons olive oil
1 cup dry bread crumbs
2 tablespoons all-purpose flour, approximately
¼ teaspoon sugar
¼ teaspoon freshly grated nutmeg
Salt
Freshly ground white pepper
2 tablespoons brandy

UTENSILS

14- to 16-inch wok or Dutch oven
13 x 9-inch baking dish
Large mixing bowl
Small bowl, plus 1 additional (if using dried sage)
Salad spinner (optional)

Measuring cups and spoons
Chef's knife
Paring knife
2 wooden spoons or metal wok spatulas
Slotted spoon
2 metal spatulas
Zester (optional)
Nutmeg grater
Meat pounder or rolling pin

START-TO-FINISH STEPS

1. Follow turkey recipe steps 1 through 8.
2. While turkey is baking, follow broccoli recipe steps 1 through 6.
3. Follow turkey recipe step 9 and serve with broccoli.

RECIPES

Stuffed Paillard of Turkey

Small bunch fresh chives, or 2-ounce package frozen
Small bunch fresh sage, or 1 teaspoon dried
¼ pound baked ham, unsliced
1 pound ground turkey
¼ teaspoon freshly grated nutmeg
1 teaspoon salt
¼ teaspoon freshly ground white pepper
2 tablespoons brandy
2 eggs
2½-pound turkey breast, skinned and boned (about 1½ pounds meat, in one piece)
2 tablespoons all-purpose flour, approximately
1 cup dry bread crumbs
1 teaspoon cream or milk
2 tablespoons unsalted butter, approximately
Small bunch watercress for garnish (optional)

1. Place rack in upper third of oven and preheat oven to 450 degrees.
2. Wash fresh chives and fresh sage, if using, and dry with paper towels. Chop enough chives to measure 3 tablespoons; chop enough sage to measure 1 tablespoon. Or, if using dried sage, place in small bowl and crush with back of wooden spoon. Cut ham into ¼-inch dice.
3. In large mixing bowl, combine diced ham, ground turkey, chives, sage, nutmeg, salt, pepper, and brandy. Separate 1 egg, dropping yolk into ground turkey mixture and

reserving white for another use. With your fingers, mix ingredients in bowl until well combined. You will have about 2 cups of filling.

4. Rinse turkey breast under cold running water and dry with paper towels. Pry apart outer and inner sections of turkey breast with your fingers (the 2 sections will separate easily). Place inner section between 2 sheets of waxed paper and pound gently with meat pounder or rolling pin to ½- to ¾-inch thickness. Repeat with outer section (the outer piece will be somewhat larger).

5. Lay larger piece out flat and, starting at wider end, spread evenly with filling, covering all except half of "tail" section, or the part the smaller piece will not cover. Top larger piece with smaller piece and fold end of tail over to enclose the filling. You should have a teardrop-shaped sandwich of roughly even thickness. Dust paillard lightly all over with flour.

6. Spread bread crumbs on large sheet of waxed paper. Combine remaining whole egg and cream in small bowl and beat with fork until well blended. Gently rub egg mixture over paillard to coat evenly. Coat paillard with bread crumbs, pressing to help crumbs adhere; let rest a minute or two, then press remaining crumbs into any damp spots that may appear.

7. Butter baking dish. Using 2 metal spatulas, transfer paillard to dish and dot with 2 tablespoons butter. Reduce oven temperature to 425 degrees and bake paillard about 25 minutes, or until crust is browned and crisp and juices run clear when meat is pierced with point of a sharp knife.

8. Meanwhile, wash watercress, if using, and dry in salad spinner or with paper towels. Remove stems and discard. Wrap in paper towels and refrigerate until ready to serve.

9. Transfer paillard to serving platter or carving board and cut into ½-inch-thick slices. Garnish platter with watercress, if desired, and serve.

Stir-Fried Broccoli with Red Bell Pepper and Lemon

Medium-size red bell pepper
1 lemon
Large clove garlic
2 large bunches broccoli (about 2½ pounds total weight)
2 tablespoons unsalted butter
2 tablespoons olive oil
¼ teaspoon sugar
1 teaspoon salt

1. Wash bell pepper and lemon, and dry with paper towel. Halve, core, and seed pepper. Cut into ¼-inch-wide strips; set aside. Avoiding white pith, grate zest from lemon. Juice lemon to make 1 tablespoon; set aside. Bruise garlic under flat blade of chef's knife; peel but leave in one piece.

2. Trim off tough, woody lower stems from broccoli. If skin is thick and tough, peel upper stems. Cut off florets and cut stem pieces into ¼-inch-thick slices.

3. Combine butter and oil in wok or Dutch oven over very low heat. Add garlic and gently sauté, uncovered, 3 to 4 minutes, or until soft and golden.

4. With slotted spoon remove garlic from pan and discard. Add lemon zest, raise heat to medium, and sauté, stirring, 2 to 3 minutes, or until zest is lightly browned and fragrant.

5. Add broccoli and bell pepper strips to pan, raise heat to high, and stir fry, sprinkling water carefully over broccoli and pepper strips to prevent sticking and browning, if necessary, until broccoli is bright green and crisp-tender, 6 to 8 minutes.

6. Stir in sugar, salt, and lemon juice. Taste and adjust seasoning. Turn broccoli into serving bowl.

ADDED TOUCH

Adjust the amounts of sugar and honey to suit your taste, remembering that the compote should be a bit tart to contrast with the ice cream. If fresh or frozen whole cranberries are unavailable, you can substitute 3 cups canned whole cranberry sauce, omitting the sugar and adding a squeeze of lemon juice if the honey makes the sauce too sweet.

Vanilla Sundaes with Cranberry Compote

12-ounce package fresh cranberries
½ cup blanched slivered almonds for topping (optional)
½ cup sugar, approximately
½ cup mild-flavored honey, approximately
⅓ cup golden rum
1½ pints top-quality vanilla ice cream

1. Preheat oven to 350 degrees.

2. Place cranberries in colander and rinse thoroughly under cold running water. Remove stems and any bruised, discolored, or underripe berries.

3. Place almonds in 9-inch pie plate and toast in oven, shaking pan occasionally to prevent scorching, 5 to 8 minutes, or until golden.

4. In medium-size heavy-gauge saucepan, combine cranberries, 1 cup water, and sugar and honey to taste over low heat and cook, stirring, 3 to 5 minutes, or until berries begin to pop and sugar is dissolved.

5. Raise heat to medium-high and simmer berries in syrup, stirring frequently, about 10 to 12 minutes, or until sauce thickens.

6. In small saucepan, gently heat rum over very low heat 30 to 45 seconds; do *not* boil.

7. Divide ice cream among 4 individual dessert bowls. Transfer hot cranberry compote to flameproof serving bowl and top with rum. Averting your face, carefully ignite rum. Before flame totally subsides, ladle cranberry compote over each serving of ice cream and top with toasted slivered almonds, if desired. Serve remaining cranberry compote on the side for guests to help themselves.

LEFTOVER SUGGESTION

Leftover *paillard* is delicious served cold as pâté or as a sandwich filling with tomatoes.

Squash and Corn Soup
Deluxe Turkey Tacos

For a festive Mexican meal serve tacos with a colorful variety of filling ingredients and a squash and corn soup.

If you want an authentic Mexican flavor in the filling for the tacos, use dried hot *pasilla* chilies rather than mild Anaheim chilies. These long, thin, wrinkly, almost black chilies are available at Mexican groceries in cellophane packets. Wipe off any surface dust and then toast them 3 to 4 minutes in an ungreased skillet to intensify their flavor and crisp them. When cool, pulverize the chilies in the container of a blender. Use 2 teaspoons ground *pasilla* (reserve extra ground *pasilla* in a tightly capped container), omit the chili powder, triple the garlic, double the cumin, and use ½ teaspoon dried oregano and ¼ teaspoon ground cloves.

Charring the tomato skins over a flame adds a rich smoky flavor to the taco filling. If you have an electric stove, preheat the broiler and grill the tomatoes, turning them until they are blackened evenly. If you would rather not char the skins, peel the tomatoes before using.

WHAT TO DRINK

The best foil for these bright flavors is a soft and fruity well-chilled white wine. Try a good Italian Orvieto or one of the drier Chenin Blancs from California. Alternatively, serve dark Mexican or Japanese beer.

SHOPPING LIST AND STAPLES

1½ pounds uncooked skinless, boneless turkey thigh meat
3 large ears fresh corn, or 10-ounce package frozen kernels
3 small yellow summer squash (about ¾ pound total weight)
2 large onions
Medium-size ripe avocado
Large head romaine lettuce
2 medium-size firm ripe tomatoes (about ¾ pound total weight)
1 large or 2 medium-size fresh green Anaheim chilies, or 1 small green bell pepper
Small bunch scallions
Small clove garlic
Small bunch fresh coriander
3½ cups chicken stock, preferably homemade (see page 11), or canned
½ pint light cream or half-and-half
8-ounce container plain yogurt or sour cream
3 tablespoons unsalted butter
½ pound Monterey Jack, Muenster, or mild Cheddar cheese
½ cup vegetable oil, approximately
2 tablespoons lard or corn oil
7½-ounce jar large, pitted black olives
10-ounce can Mexican hot sauce
8 fresh corn tortillas, or 1 package frozen
2-ounce jar pine nuts
1 tablespoon medium-hot chili powder
½ teaspoon ground cumin

1 teaspoon hot red pepper flakes, approximately (if not using fresh chilies)
Pinch of dried oregano
Pinch of ground cloves
Pinch of sugar
Salt

UTENSILS

Food processor (optional)
Blender
Stockpot or large saucepan
Large heavy-gauge skillet
Medium-size skillet
9-inch pie pan
8 x 8-inch baking dish
Heatproof platter
Large bowl
Measuring cups and spoons
Chef's knife
Paring knife
2 cooking spoons, preferably stainless steel
Long-handled double-pronged fork
Grater (if not using processor)

START-TO-FINISH STEPS

One hour ahead: If using frozen tortillas for tacos or frozen corn for soup, set out to thaw.

1. Peel and chop 2 large onions for soup and tacos recipes.
2. Follow soup recipe steps 1 through 3.
3. Follow tacos recipe steps 1 through 7.
4. Follow soup recipe step 4.
5. Follow tacos recipe steps 8 through 13.
6. Follow soup recipe steps 5 through 7.
7. Follow tacos recipe steps 14 and 15, soup recipe step 8, and serve.

RECIPES

Squash and Corn Soup

3 tablespoons unsalted butter
1 cup chopped onion
3 small yellow summer squash (about ¾ pound total weight)
3 large ears fresh corn, or 10-ounce package frozen kernels
3½ cups chicken stock
Pinch of sugar
½ cup light cream or half-and-half
Small bunch fresh coriander
Salt (optional)

1. Melt butter in stockpot or large saucepan over medium heat. Add onion and sauté, stirring occasionally, about 5 to 8 minutes, until onion is soft and beginning to turn golden brown around the edges.

2. While onion is cooking, wash squash under cold running water and dry with paper towels. Trim off ends and coarsely chop enough squash to measure 2¼ cups. If using fresh corn, remove husks and silk from corn and discard. With chef's knife, trim each stem end so upended ears will rest flat against bottom of baking dish. Holding 1 ear of corn upright, press base against dish, and cut off kernels by pressing knife blade against cob and slicing downward. Turn cob and repeat process until all kernels are removed. Scrape ear with dull side of knife blade to press out juice. Repeat for remaining ears.

3. Add vegetables to stockpot and stir to combine. Stir in stock and sugar and bring soup to a boil. Lower heat, cover, and simmer gently 30 to 35 minutes, or until vegetables are thoroughly cooked.

4. Remove soup from heat and set aside to cool slightly.

5. Transfer half the soup to food processor or blender and purée. Transfer purée to large bowl and repeat for remaining soup. Return soup to stockpot and stir in cream. Place pot over medium heat and slowly bring soup to a simmer, stirring frequently, about 5 minutes.

6. Meanwhile, wash coriander and dry with paper towels. Coarsely chop enough coriander to measure ½ to ¾ cup.

7. Taste soup and add salt, if desired. Remove pot from heat and cover to keep warm.

8. When ready to serve stir in coriander, divide soup among 4 bowls, and serve.

Deluxe Turkey Tacos

Small clove garlic
1½ pounds uncooked skinless, boneless turkey thigh meat
1 large or 2 medium-size fresh green Anaheim chilies, or 1 small green bell pepper
2 tablespoons lard or corn oil
1 cup chopped onion
2 medium-size firm ripe tomatoes (about ¾ pound total weight)
1 tablespoon medium-hot chili powder
½ teaspoon ground cumin
Pinch of dried oregano
Pinch of ground cloves
½ to 1 teaspoon hot red pepper flakes (if not using fresh chilies)
½ cup pine nuts
Large head romaine lettuce
½ pound Monterey Jack, Muenster, or mild Cheddar cheese
Small bunch scallions
Medium-size ripe avocado
½ cup large, pitted black olives
½ cup vegetable oil, approximately
8 fresh corn tortillas, or 1 package frozen, thawed
1 cup plain yogurt or sour cream
1 cup Mexican hot sauce

1. Preheat oven to 350 degrees.

2. Peel and finely mince garlic. Wash turkey and dry with paper towels. Coarsely chop turkey. Wash chilies and dry with paper towels. Halve, core, and seed chilies; dice enough to measure ⅓ cup.

3. Heat lard or oil in large heavy-gauge skillet over medium heat. Add onion and sauté, stirring occasionally, about 5 to 8 minutes, or until onion is soft and starting to turn golden brown around the edges.

4. While onion is cooking, place 1 tomato on long-handled two-prong fork. Roast over high gas flame, turning tomato to roast evenly, 5 to 7 minutes, or until skin blackens. Repeat with remaining tomato. Set tomatoes aside to cool; do not remove blackened skins.

5. Add turkey, garlic, chili powder, cumin, oregano, cloves, and red pepper flakes if using (do not add fresh chilies at this point) to onion mixture in skillet and stir to combine. Raise heat slightly and cook, stirring frequently, until turkey starts to brown on the outside, 3 to 5 minutes.

6. Meanwhile, core and chop roasted tomatoes, blackened skins included. You should have about 1½ cups tomatoes.

7. Stir tomatoes into turkey mixture, raise heat to high, and cook, stirring occasionally, until meat is thoroughly cooked and mixture is very thick, about 15 minutes. There should be just enough sauce to bind mixture together.

8. Place pine nuts in pie pan and toast in oven, shaking pan occasionally to prevent scorching, 5 to 8 minutes, or until golden.

9. Meanwhile, wash lettuce and dry with paper towels. Stack leaves together and, using chef's knife, cut enough lettuce crosswise into ⅛-inch-wide shreds to measure 5 to 6 cups. Grate cheese in food processor or on coarse side of grater to measure about 2 cups. Wash scallions and dry with paper towels; trim off ends and chop coarsely.

10. Remove nuts from oven and set aside to cool; reduce oven temperature to 200 degrees. Line heatproof platter with paper towels.

11. Remove turkey mixture from heat and keep covered.

12. Halve avocado lengthwise; twist halves in opposite directions to separate. Remove pit and discard. Peel the avocado and cut into ½-inch dice. Coarsely chop olives. Place yogurt or sour cream and hot sauce in small serving bowls.

13. Fill medium-size skillet with ½ inch vegetable oil and heat until oil is shimmering but not smoking. Lightly fry each tortilla on one side, and while it is still pliable, turn over and fold in half. Fry folded tortilla on both sides, turning until crisp; transfer to paper-towel-lined heatproof platter. Repeat for remaining tortillas; place in oven to keep warm.

14. Return turkey mixture to medium heat, stir in chilies and cook just until they turn bright green, about 4 minutes.

15. Add pine nuts to turkey mixture and stir to combine. Divide filling among taco shells and top with any combination of shredded lettuce, grated cheese, chopped scallions, chopped olives, and diced avocado. Transfer tacos to dinner plates. Serve with bowls of yogurt or sour cream and hot sauce.

Turkey-Spinach Meatballs with Noodles
Fresh Tomato Salad with Tarragon

For a casual supper, turkey meatballs flecked with fresh spinach are heaped on a bed of green noodles. The salad of vine-ripened tomatoes is drizzled with dressing and sprinkled with fresh tarragon.

Fresh spinach and tomatoes are highly recommended for this menu. If you must use frozen spinach, substitute one package, fully thawed and finely chopped. Sauté the spinach in a nonaluminum pan.

The fresh tomato salad also calls for *pumate* (Italian sun-dried tomatoes with a highly concentrated flavor) as an optional addition to the dressing. *Pumate* are sold loose or oil-packed in jars at specialty food shops and Italian groceries; you will need the oil-packed type for this recipe. Although *pumate* are expensive, they are well worth serving as a special treat. Instead of a tomato salad, you might try fresh asparagus or artichokes.

WHAT TO DRINK

Choose a flavorful California Chardonnay or Sauvignon Blanc (especially one blended with some Sémillon) or an Alsatian or Italian Pinot Blanc for this menu.

SHOPPING LIST AND STAPLES

1½ pounds ground turkey
½ pound fresh spinach
4 large ripe tomatoes (about 2 pounds total weight)
2 cloves garlic
1 bunch fresh tarragon, or 1¼ teaspoons dried
Large juice orange
1 lemon
2 eggs
½ pint heavy cream
4 tablespoons unsalted butter
8-ounce container ricotta cheese
2 ounces Parmesan cheese
¾ pound fresh wide spinach noodles (tagliatelle), or ½ pound dried
½ cup chicken stock, preferably homemade (see page 11), or canned
2 tablespoons virgin olive oil, plus ¼ cup, approximately (optional)
6½-ounce jar oil-packed sun-dried tomatoes (optional)
½ cup all-purpose flour, approximately
½ teaspoon freshly grated nutmeg
½ teaspoon cracked black pepper
Salt
⅓ cup Marsala

33

UTENSILS

Food processor (optional)
Stockpot
2 large or medium-size heavy-gauge skillets or sauté
  pans, 1 nonaluminum and 1 with cover
15 x 10-inch cookie sheet
Heatproof platter
9-inch pie pan
Large mixing bowl
Small bowl
Colander
Measuring cups and spoons
Chef's knife
Paring knife
Wooden spoon
Whisk
Nutmeg grater
Grater (if not using processor)
Citrus juicer

START-TO-FINISH STEPS

1. Follow meatballs recipe steps 1 through 9.
2. Follow salad recipe steps 1 through 5.
3. Follow meatballs recipe steps 10 through 15.
4. Follow salad recipe step 6, meatballs recipe step 16, and
serve.

RECIPES

Turkey-Spinach Meatballs with Noodles

½ pound fresh spinach
2 ounces Parmesan cheese
2 cloves garlic
4 tablespoons unsalted butter
1½ pounds ground turkey
½ teaspoon freshly grated nutmeg
6 tablespoons ricotta cheese
1 teaspoon salt
½ teaspoon cracked black pepper
2 eggs
½ cup all-purpose flour, approximately
2 tablespoons virgin olive oil
⅓ cup Marsala
¾ pound fresh wide spinach noodles (tagliatelle), or
  ½ pound dried

½ cup chicken stock
¾ cup heavy cream

1. Rinse spinach thoroughly. Remove tough stems and discard. Reserve 8 small leaves for garnish and coarsely chop enough of the remaining leaves to measure 6 cups.
2. Grate enough Parmesan in food processor or with grater to measure 6 tablespoons. Peel and finely mince garlic.
3. Heat 1 tablespoon butter in large nonaluminum skillet over medium heat. Add spinach and sauté, stirring frequently, until liquid has evaporated, 6 to 7 minutes.
4. While spinach is cooking, combine turkey, Parmesan, nutmeg, garlic, ricotta, salt, and pepper in large bowl. Separate eggs, adding yolks to bowl and reserving whites for another use. Stir mixture just until combined.
5. When spinach is cooked, remove from heat to cool.
6. Preheat oven to 200 degrees. Line cookie sheet with waxed paper. Place about ⅓ cup flour in pie pan.
7. Gradually add cooked spinach to turkey mixture, stirring just until spinach is evenly distributed. With floured hands, divide mixture into 16 or more portions and roll between palms of hands to form balls. As each meatball is formed, roll it lightly in flour and transfer to prepared cookie sheet. Place heatproof platter in oven to warm.
8. Place 2 dry heavy-gauge skillets over medium heat. When skillets are hot, divide remaining 3 tablespoons butter and the oil between the 2 pans. Tilt and rotate each pan to completely cover bottoms with fat. When fat is hot and just starting to brown, add meatballs and fry, shaking pans and turning meatballs occasionally, 15 to 20 minutes, or until brown and juices run clear when meatballs are pierced with a sharp knife.
9. Meanwhile, bring 3 quarts of water to a boil in stockpot over high heat.
10. When meatballs are done, transfer to warm platter, cover loosely with foil, and set aside.
11. Pour fat from one skillet into skillet with cover. Add Marsala to empty skillet and scrape up browned bits clinging to bottom of pan; set aside.
12. Set skillet with fat over low heat. Stir in 2 tablespoons flour and cook, stirring briskly, 5 minutes.
13. Add noodles to boiling water and cook 4 to 6 minutes for fresh, 8 to 12 minutes for dried, or until *al dente*.
14. Add stock to skillet with fat in a slow, steady stream, whisking briskly until totally incorporated. Add contents of pan with Marsala to pan with stock and whisk until

blended. Stir in cream, raise heat to medium, and cook, stirring constantly, 3 to 4 minutes, or until sauce is thick enough to coat back of spoon. Remove pan from heat, cover, and keep warm until ready to serve.

15. Turn noodles into colander and drain.

16. Divide noodles among 4 dinner plates and top each with meatballs and a generous spoonful of sauce. Garnish each serving with 2 spinach leaves.

Fresh Tomato Salad with Tarragon

1 bunch fresh tarragon, or 1¼ teaspoons dried, crumbled
Large juice orange
1 lemon
6½-ounce jar oil-packed sun-dried tomatoes (optional)
¼ cup virgin olive oil, approximately (optional)
Pinch of salt
4 large ripe tomatoes (about 2 pounds total weight)

1. Wash fresh tarragon, if using, and dry with paper towels. Reserve 20 sprigs for garnish and mince enough to measure 1 tablespoon.

2. Squeeze enough orange to measure ¼ cup juice. Squeeze enough lemon to measure 1 tablespoon juice.

3. Drain and reserve ¼ cup oil from sun-dried tomatoes, if using; if necessary, add enough virgin olive oil to measure ¼ cup. Or, measure ¼ cup virgin olive oil. Mince enough sun-dried tomatoes, if using, to measure 1 tablespoon.

4. For dressing, combine orange juice, lemon juice, oil, minced sun-dried tomatoes, and salt in small bowl. With fork, beat dressing until well blended.

5. Wash tomatoes and dry with paper towels. Core and cut into ¼-inch-thick slices. Divide among 4 salad plates and set aside.

6. When ready to serve, stir dressing to recombine, pour over tomatoes, and garnish with tarragon sprigs.

ADDED TOUCH

For this refreshing *galette*, or tart-like cake, use firm pears.

Pear Galette

Crust:
Large lemon
1½ cups all-purpose flour
2 tablespoons vanilla sugar or granulated sugar
1 stick lightly salted butter, well chilled
1 egg yolk

Filling:
2 pounds firm, ripe pears, such as Bosc or d'Anjou
1 cup granulated sugar
½ cup heavy cream
¼ cup sour cream
3 tablespoons pear brandy or Cognac

1. For crust, wash lemon and, with paring knife, cut two 3-inch-long, ¼-inch-wide strips of peel; set aside. Grate remaining zest and reserve. Squeeze lemon to measure about ¼ cup juice and combine with 1 quart cold water in large mixing bowl; set aside.

2. Combine flour, sugar, and lemon zest in food processor fitted with steel blade and pulse once or twice to mix. Cut butter into 8 pieces, add to processor, and process just until mixture forms coarse crumbs. Add egg yolk and process about 30 seconds, or until dough forms and pulls away from sides of bowl. If it does not, continue to process, adding cold water 1 teaspoon at a time, just until dough gathers on blade. Form dough into a flat round cake, wrap in plastic, and refrigerate until firm, about 30 minutes.

3. For filling: Peel, halve, and core pears, placing halves in bowl of lemon water to prevent discoloration.

4. Pour 2 cups lemon water into shallow nonaluminum baking dish, add 1 cup sugar and reserved strips of lemon peel, and bring to a simmer over medium heat, stirring until sugar is dissolved. Add pears and poach 10 to 15 minutes, or until transparent and just tender. With slotted spoon, transfer pears to plate and set aside.

5. Pour 1 cup of the cooking syrup into small saucepan and bring to a boil over high heat. Boil about 10 minutes, or until syrup is very thick and reduced to ½ cup. Set aside.

6. Butter a 9-inch tart pan or pie pan. Roll out dough between 2 sheets of waxed paper into ⅛-inch-thick circle and fit into pan. Line crust with foil, weight with pie weights or dried beans, and bake 15 minutes.

7. Remove weights and foil, return crust to oven, and bake another 10 minutes, or until crust is golden brown.

8. Remove crust from oven and set aside to cool.

9. In medium-size bowl, beat heavy cream with electric mixer at high speed until stiff peaks form. In small bowl, combine sour cream, pear brandy or Cognac, and 2 tablespoons reduced syrup, and beat until blended. Gently fold sour cream mixture into the whipped cream.

10. Cut pears lengthwise into ¼-inch-thick slices, arrange them in a pinwheel pattern in baked crust, and drizzle with reduced syrup. Cut galette into wedges and serve with brandy-cream topping.

Douglas Oaks

MENU 1 (Right)
Turkey Wellington
Sautéed Romaine with Romano Cheese,
Mushrooms, and Onions

MENU 2
**Turkey Breast with Spinach and Scallop Stuffing
and Pineapple Chutney Sauce**
Warm French Bread

MENU 3
Cucumber Soup
Sautéed Turkey Cutlets with Herb-Caper Sauce
Asparagus with Cherry Tomatoes and Cashews

Whether cooking for friends or for himself, Douglas Oaks enjoys opening his refrigerator and creating a complete meal with whatever is on hand. His larder is generally well stocked with ready-to-cook meats that fit his requirements for effortless preparation. He particularly likes turkey for its versatility—especially turkey breasts, which can be presented in many guises, as he demonstrates here.

For the festive entrée in Menu 1, he covers turkey cutlets with *pâté de foie gras*, wraps them in prosciutto, then bakes each cutlet in a puff-pastry shell. Romaine lettuce filled with grated Romano cheese and chopped mushrooms and onions goes well with the turkey.

He again performs wonders with a turkey breast in Menu 2. He makes a pocket in the breast, lines it with carrot strips, and stuffs it with scallops, mushrooms, and spinach. Just before serving, he slices the stuffed breast into medallions, then spoons a pineapple chutney sauce over each portion.

In Menu 3, Douglas Oaks shows that turkey is also a viable and inexpensive alternative to veal. For the entrée, he briefly sautées turkey cutlets in anchovy-flavored butter—as one might do with veal cutlets—and serves them with a Hollandaise-type sauce garnished with crab meat.

Turkey cutlets wrapped in golden pastry crusts make a sumptuous entrée when served with romaine leaves filled with cheese, mushrooms, and onions. For an elegant touch, pour the wine from a crystal decanter.

Turkey Breast with Spinach and Scallop Stuffing and Pineapple Chutney Sauce
Warm French Bread

Slices of turkey breast with a mosaic-like stuffing are best set off by solid-color plates and a simple fruit garnish.

The turkey breast is stuffed with a medley of ingredients, including sweet bay scallops. Prized for their tenderness, these small scallops are creamy ivory and about half an inch in diameter. When perfectly fresh, they are translucent; avoid any that are opaque, which indicates age or prior freezing. If you must purchase large scallops, cut them into ½-inch cubes before adding them to the stuffing. Two generous slices of the stuffed breast are a complete meal when served with warm French bread.

WHAT TO DRINK

A firm, acidic white wine such as a California Sauvignon Blanc or an Alsatian Gewürztraminer would be good with this menu. Or serve sparkling water.

SHOPPING LIST AND STAPLES

2-pound section of boneless, skinless turkey breast
½ pound bay scallops
¼ pound bacon (about 4 slices)
Medium-size onion
2 medium-size carrots

½ pound fresh cultivated mushrooms
Small bunch fresh parsley
1 clove garlic
1 orange (optional)
1 kiwi fruit (optional)
1 stick unsalted butter
Two 10-ounce packages frozen chopped spinach
2 cups chicken stock, preferably homemade (see page 11), or canned
8-ounce can unsweetened crushed pineapple
8-ounce jar sweet chutney
3 tablespoons all-purpose flour
1 loaf French bread
¼ teaspoon fennel seeds
¼ teaspoon thyme
Salt
Freshly ground white pepper
½ cup dry white wine

UTENSILS

Food processor (optional)
Medium-size sauté pan or skillet

Small heavy-gauge saucepan
Small saucepan
12 x 9-inch roasting pan
Large strainer
Fine strainer
Measuring cups and spoons
Chef's knife
Paring knife
Rubber spatula
2 wooden spoons
Mortar and pestle (optional)
Vegetable peeler
Rolling pin (if not using mortar and pestle)

START-TO-FINISH STEPS

One hour ahead: Set frozen spinach out to thaw for stuffing recipe.

1. Peel and halve onion. Chop one half for turkey recipe and quarter other half for stuffing recipe.
2. Follow turkey recipe step 1 and stuffing recipe steps 1 through 8.
3. Follow turkey recipe steps 2 through 14 and serve.

RECIPES

Turkey Breast with Spinach and Scallop Stuffing and Pineapple Chutney Sauce

2 medium-size carrots
2-pound section of boneless, skinless turkey breast
Salt
Freshly ground white pepper
Spinach and Scallop Stuffing (see following recipe)
1 stick unsalted butter
½ medium-size onion, chopped
2 tablespoons sweet chutney
1 cup unsweetened crushed pineapple
1 orange (optional)
1 kiwi fruit (optional)
3 tablespoons all-purpose flour
1 loaf French bread
½ cup dry white wine
2 cups chicken stock

1. Preheat oven to 400 degrees.
2. Peel and trim carrots. Cut carrots into 1½-inch-long pieces; halve pieces and cut into ¼-inch julienne.
3. Lay turkey breast flat on work surface, and cut a pocket for stuffing three quarters of the way through the breast, being careful not to cut completely through.
4. Lightly season pocket with salt and pepper. Line pocket with carrots and then fill cavity with spinach and scallop stuffing, taking care to keep the carrot lining between turkey meat and stuffing.
5. In small heavy-gauge saucepan, melt butter over low heat.

6. Place breast in roasting pan. Pour melted butter over breast and sprinkle with salt and pepper. Sprinkle chopped onion and chutney around breast. Drain pineapple and add solids to pan. Place pan in oven and roast breast, stirring onion and chutney occasionally, 30 to 35 minutes, or until juices run clear when breast is pierced with tip of a sharp knife.
7. Wash orange, if using, and dry with paper towel. Cut four ¼-inch-thick rounds crosswise from center of orange; set aside. Peel and halve kiwi, if using. Cut one half of kiwi into 4 wedges; reserve remaining half for another use.
8. When breast is done, transfer to platter and cover loosely with foil to keep warm until ready to serve. Reduce oven temperature to 200 degrees.
9. Place roasting pan over medium heat and stir, scraping up browned bits clinging to bottom of pan. Then sauté onion and chutney 2 to 3 minutes, or until a residue of browned particles has formed on bottom of pan.
10. Add flour to roasting pan and cook, stirring constantly, another 2 to 3 minutes.
11. Place bread in oven to warm.
12. Add wine and stock to roasting pan and cook, stirring, 2 to 3 minutes, or until sauce thickens.
13. Pour sauce through fine strainer set over small saucepan, pressing with back of spoon to extract as much liquid as possible. Adjust seasoning and reheat sauce, if necessary.
14. Cut breast into eight ½-inch-thick medallions and divide among 4 dinner plates. Top each serving with sauce and garnish plate with a slice of orange and a wedge of kiwi, if desired. Serve with warm bread.

Spinach and Scallop Stuffing

½ pound fresh cultivated mushrooms
1 clove garlic
Two 10-ounce packages frozen chopped spinach, thawed
Small bunch fresh parsley
½ medium-size onion, quartered
¼ pound bacon (about 4 slices)
¼ teaspoon fennel seeds
½ pound bay scallops
¼ teaspoon thyme
Salt
Freshly ground white pepper

1. Wipe mushrooms with damp paper towels. Peel garlic. Place thawed spinach in large strainer to drain. Wash parsley and dry with paper towels; chop enough to measure ¼ cup and set aside.
2. In food processor fitted with steel blade, chop garlic. Add onion and bacon, and process just until onion and bacon are chopped. Or, using chef's knife, finely mince garlic, chop onion, and cut bacon into ½-inch dice.
3. Crush fennel seeds in mortar with pestle or place between 2 sheets of waxed paper and crush with rolling pin.
4. Rinse scallops under cold running water, dry with paper towels, and set aside.

5. Place garlic, onion, and bacon in medium-size sauté pan or skillet over medium-high heat and sauté, stirring occasionally, about 5 minutes, or until onion begins to brown.
6. Meanwhile, place drained spinach between double thickness of paper towels and press out excess moisture. Transfer spinach to food processor, add mushrooms, and chop together finely; or, chop finely with chef's knife.
7. Add spinach and mushrooms, parsley, fennel seeds, thyme, and salt and pepper to taste to bacon mixture in skillet and stir just until ingredients are combined.
8. Remove skillet from heat and gently fold in scallops; set aside.

ADDED TOUCHES

In this unusual salad, leaves of Belgian endive surround the marinated broccoli. If the endive tastes slightly bitter, blanch the leaves quickly to improve the flavor; then refresh under cold running water.

Marinated Broccoli and Belgian Endive Salad

1 head broccoli
1 red bell pepper
4 ounces feta cheese
¼ cup pitted black olives
½ cup olive oil
2 tablespoons red wine vinegar
½ teaspoon thyme
1 tablespoon chopped parsley
Salt
Freshly ground white pepper
2 heads Belgian endive

1. Wash and trim broccoli. Cut into florets.
2. In saucepan large enough to accommodate steamer, bring 2 cups water to a boil over high heat. Add broccoli, cover, lower heat to medium, and steam broccoli 4 to 5 minutes, or until crisp-tender.
3. Meanwhile, wash red pepper and dry with paper towel. Halve, core, and seed pepper. Dice enough pepper to measure ½ cup and place in large bowl.
4. Transfer broccoli to colander and place under cold running water to cool.
5. Crumble cheese and slice olives. Add to bowl with diced pepper.
6. Drain broccoli and dry with paper towels. Add broccoli to bowl.
7. For dressing, combine oil, vinegar, thyme, parsley, and salt and pepper to taste in small bowl and whisk vigorously until blended.
8. Pour dressing over salad and toss to combine. Cover bowl with plastic wrap and refrigerate until ready to serve.
9. Wipe endive clean with a damp paper towel. Trim and separate leaves. Arrange leaves on serving platter in sunburst pattern.
10. Just before serving, toss salad to recombine and spoon into center of platter.

For the tenderest and lightest crêpes, allow the batter to rest for at least one hour before cooking. Crêpes may be made several hours or even days in advance. Store them on a plate, interleaved with squares of waxed paper to keep them from sticking together, and refrigerate wrapped in foil or plastic wrap. Reheat the crêpes in a warm oven before filling with the strawberries.

Strawberry Crêpes with Grand Marnier Sauce

Crêpes:
¾ cup all-purpose flour
1 egg
¼ cup sugar
1 cup heavy cream
1 tablespoon unsalted butter, melted
1 tablespoon Grand Marnier or other orange-flavored liqueur
Pinch of salt

1 pint fresh strawberries

Sauce:
2 eggs
¼ cup sugar
¼ cup heavy cream
1 tablespoon Grand Marnier

1. In medium-size bowl, combine crêpes ingredients and stir with wooden spoon until blended.
2. Pour mixture through strainer set over small bowl and set aside for at least 15 minutes.
3. Meanwhile, gently rinse strawberries under cold water and dry with paper towels. Hull berries and, if large, cut in half; set aside.
4. Preheat oven to 200 degrees.
5. Set small nonstick skillet or omelet pan over medium heat. When hot, ladle just enough batter into pan to cover bottom and cook about 30 seconds, or until lightly browned. Using plastic spatula, flip crêpe and cook another 30 seconds. As each crêpe is cooked, transfer to heatproof platter and keep warm in oven until ready to serve. Repeat with remaining batter until you have 8 small crêpes.
6. In bottom of double boiler, bring 1 quart of water just to a simmer over medium heat.
7. For sauce, separate eggs, placing yolks in nonaluminum top of double boiler, off heat, and reserving whites for another use. Add 1 tablespoon water to yolks and whisk until frothy.
8. Place yolks over, not in, barely simmering water and whisk vigorously until stiff.
9. Gradually add sugar and whisk until blended. Still whisking, slowly add cream and continue to whisk 2 minutes, or until sauce is smooth.
10. Remove sauce from heat and stir in Grand Marnier.
11. Divide strawberries among crêpes and roll up to enclose berries. Transfer crêpes to plates, top with Grand Marnier sauce, and serve.

Cucumber Soup
Sautéed Turkey Cutlets with Herb-Caper Sauce
Asparagus with Cherry Tomatoes and Cashews

Cucumber soup precedes the entrée of turkey cutlets topped with herb sauce and crab meat. Sautéed vegetables add color.

The refreshing cucumber soup is a perfect introduction to this meal and is delicious either hot or chilled. For cold soup, bring the puréed ingredients to a boil, then remove from the heat and pour into a serving bowl. At this point, add *cold* heavy cream to the soup and chill for 20 to 30 minutes. If you prefer a thinner consistency, add more heavy cream just before serving.

Ideal for a last-minute spring or summer dinner, the turkey cutlets sauté quickly over high heat. They are ready when both sides are golden and the meat feels firm but not hard. The cutlets can be served on slices of toasted French bread or on garlic toasts. If cherry tomatoes are unavailable, use a red bell pepper cut into ¼-inch-wide strips.

WHAT TO DRINK

With this dinner, the cook suggests serving a soft, slightly sweet white wine such as a German Piesporter. Or, you might try a California Riesling or a dry white Graves or Sancerre.

SHOPPING LIST AND STAPLES

Eight ½-inch-thick turkey cutlets (about 2 pounds total weight)
¼ pound lump crab meat, fresh or frozen (optional)
1 pound asparagus
1 pint cherry tomatoes
4 small cucumbers
Medium-size potato
Medium-size onion
Small bunch fresh chives or 2-ounce container frozen
Small bunch fresh tarragon, or 1 teaspoon dried
1 clove garlic
Small lemon
2 cups chicken stock, preferably homemade (see page 11), or canned
3 eggs
½ pint heavy cream
3 sticks unsalted butter
2 ounces Parmesan cheese
4 tablespoons Dijon mustard
2-ounce jar capers

43

2-ounce tin anchovy fillets
1 cup all-purpose flour, approximately
1 large loaf French bread
¼-pound package whole salted cashews
½ teaspoon dried thyme
1 bay leaf
Salt
2 peppercorns
Freshly ground white pepper
2 tablespoons dry white wine

UTENSILS

Food processor or blender
Large heavy-gauge skillet
Medium-size saucepan
2 small saucepans
Large sauté pan with cover
Nonaluminum double boiler
Flameproof baking pan
Platter
9-inch pie pan
Small bowl
Strainer
Fine sieve or cheesecloth
Butter warmer (if not using small saucepan)
Measuring cups and spoons
Chef's knife
Paring knife
Wooden spoon
Metal spatula
Whisk
Metal tongs
Pastry brush
Vegetable peeler
Grater (if not using food processor)

START-TO-FINISH STEPS

One hour ahead: If using frozen crab meat to garnish turkey cutlets, set out 2 ounces to thaw.

Fifteen minutes ahead: In small saucepan or butter warmer, clarify butter (see page 10) for turkey recipe.

1. For turkey and sauce recipes, drain 6 anchovy fillets, rinse, dry with paper towel, and mince; set aside. Peel and finely dice onion for soup and sauce recipes.
2. Follow soup recipe steps 1 through 4.
3. Follow turkey recipe steps 1 through 4.
4. Follow soup recipe step 5 and asparagus recipe step 1.
5. Follow soup recipe step 6 and turkey recipe step 5.
6. Follow soup recipe steps 7 through 9 and serve as first course.
7. Follow turkey recipe steps 6 through 9.
8. Follow sauce recipe steps 1 through 11.
9. Follow asparagus recipe steps 2 through 4.
10. Follow turkey recipe steps 10 and 11, and serve with asparagus.

44

RECIPES

Cucumber Soup

4 small cucumbers
1 clove garlic
Medium-size potato
4 tablespoons unsalted butter
½ medium-size onion, finely diced
Small bunch fresh chives or 2-ounce container frozen
2 cups chicken stock
½ cup heavy cream

1. Peel cucumbers and halve lengthwise. Scoop out seeds with teaspoon and discard. Cut into ½-inch dice. Peel and mince garlic; peel and dice potato.
2. In medium-size saucepan, heat butter over medium heat. Add onion and sauté, stirring occasionally, about 5 minutes, or just until onion begins to brown around edges. Do not allow onion to brown completely.
3. If using fresh chives, rinse and dry. Chop enough chives to measure 3 tablespoons; set aside.
4. Add cucumbers, garlic, potato, and 2 tablespoons chives to onion, and sauté, stirring occasionally, 10 to 15 minutes, or until potato is translucent.
5. Add chicken stock and bring to a boil. Reduce heat to medium-low and simmer 5 minutes.
6. Remove pan from heat and set aside to cool slightly.
7. Transfer mixture to food processor fitted with steel blade, or blender, and purée. Return soup to saucepan and simmer another 3 minutes.
8. Place cream in small bowl. Add ¼ cup soup to cream, stir to blend, and then slowly add mixture to soup, stirring continuously until blended.
9. Heat soup 1 or 2 minutes; then divide among 4 bowls, garnish with remaining chives, and serve.

Sautéed Turkey Cutlets with Herb-Caper Sauce

2 ounces Parmesan cheese
1 tablespoon tarragon leaves, or 1 teaspoon dried
Four 1-inch-thick slices French bread
Eight ½-inch-thick turkey cutlets (about 2 pounds total weight)
4 tablespoons Dijon mustard
Salt and freshly ground white pepper
1 stick unsalted butter, clarified
4 anchovy fillets, minced
1 cup all-purpose flour, approximately
2 ounces lump crab meat for garnish (optional)
Herb-Caper Sauce (see following recipe)

1. Set broiler rack 4 inches from heating element and preheat broiler. Line a platter with paper towels.
2. Grate enough Parmesan to measure 2 tablespoons.
3. If using fresh tarragon, rinse and dry with paper towels. Chop enough to measure 1 tablespoon.
4. Place French bread in flameproof baking pan and sprin-

kle each slice with ½ tablespoon Parmesan cheese. Broil 30 seconds or until lightly browned. Remove from broiler and reduce oven temperature to 200 degrees. Place toasted bread in oven to keep warm.

5. Rinse cutlets and dry with paper towels. Brush both sides with mustard and season with tarragon and salt and pepper. Pat gently to help seasoning adhere.

6. Heat half the clarified butter and anchovies in large heavy-gauge skillet over medium heat 2 or 3 minutes, or until anchovies disintegrate.

7. Meanwhile, place flour in pie pan. Dredge each cutlet in flour and shake off excess.

8. Add as many cutlets as will fit in skillet without crowding and sauté over medium-high heat 2 to 3 minutes per side, or until golden brown. Transfer to paper-towel-lined platter and keep warm in oven. Heat remaining butter and anchovies and sauté remaining cutlets 2 to 3 minutes per side. When second batch of cutlets is done, transfer to oven with first batch and keep warm until ready to serve.

9. Place crab meat, if using, in strainer and rinse under cold running water. Remove and discard any cartilage or shell fragments. Dry with paper towels.

10. Place crab meat in skillet and sauté over medium heat 2 to 3 minutes, or until heated through.

11. Place 1 slice of toasted bread on each of 4 dinner plates and top each slice with 2 cutlets. Spoon herb-caper sauce over each serving and garnish with crab meat, if desired.

Herb-Caper Sauce

2 tablespoons dry white wine
1 bay leaf
1 tablespoon finely diced onion
2 peppercorns
1 stick unsalted butter
1 tablespoon capers
Small lemon
3 eggs
2 anchovy fillets, minced

1. In small saucepan, combine wine, bay leaf, onion, and peppercorns, and bring to a boil over medium-high heat. Continue to boil 2 to 3 minutes, or until reduced by half.

2. Melt butter over low heat just until simmering.

3. Meanwhile, drain capers and chop; set aside.

4. Strain wine mixture through a fine sieve or damp cheesecloth over small bowl; set aside.

5. Remove butter from heat.

6. In bottom of double boiler, bring 1 quart of water just to a simmer over medium heat.

7. Squeeze enough lemon juice to measure 1 teaspoon into top of double boiler, off heat. Separate eggs, adding yolks to lemon juice and reserving whites for another use.

8. Place yolk mixture over, not in, barely simmering water, add 1 tablespoon water, and whisk, about 3 minutes, or until mixture has consistency of heavy cream.

9. Remove top of double boiler from heat and slowly add warm butter alternately with the strained wine mixture, whisking continuously until sauce thins.

10. Place sauce over simmering water again and continue to whisk until sauce reaches desired thickness. If sauce begins to curdle, remove from heat and continue whisking. You may also add a few drops of cold water, milk, or cream and whisk slowly until yolks begin to accept the liquid; then speed up whisking.

11. Stir in anchovies and capers, cover, and let sit over water, off heat, at least 5 to 10 minutes before serving.

Asparagus with Cherry Tomatoes and Cashews

1 pound asparagus
16 cherry tomatoes
4 tablespoons unsalted butter
½ cup whole salted cashews
½ teaspoon dried thyme

1. Wash asparagus spears and snap off tough, woody bottoms. Wash cherry tomatoes; remove stems.

2. In large sauté pan, heat butter over high heat. Add cashews and sauté, stirring, about 3 minutes, or until cashews are lightly browned.

3. Add asparagus, tomatoes, and thyme to pan, and sauté, 1 to 2 minutes, shaking pan to prevent burning.

4. Add 2 tablespoons of water, cover pan, and remove from heat. If large asparagus spears are used or if you prefer a fully cooked or soft vegetable, leave the covered pan on the burner for a minute or two before removing from heat. In either case, let vegetables stand off heat, covered, for about 5 minutes before serving.

ADDED TOUCH

A mousse is a good dessert for this menu. If hazelnuts are not available, substitute chopped pecans or walnuts.

Kahlúa and Hazelnut Mousse

2 egg yolks
⅓ cup granulated sugar
½ pint whipping cream
2 to 3 tablespoons Kahlúa, Tia Maria or other coffee-
   flavored liqueur
¼ cup chopped plus 8 whole hazelnuts

1. In small bowl, combine egg yolks and 1 tablespoon of cold water and beat with electric mixer until frothy.

2. Add sugar to egg yolks and beat until smooth. Turn mixture into large bowl. Rinse and dry small bowl.

3. In small bowl, beat ¾ cup whipping cream until stiff.

4. Add liqueur and chopped nuts to egg mixture and fold in. Gently fold in whipped cream until totally incorporated.

5. Divide mousse among individual bowls or goblets and freeze 1 to 2 hours before serving.

6. Just before serving, whip remaining cream until stiff. Top each serving of mousse with a spoonful of cream, garnish with whole nuts, and serve.

Leslee Reis

L eslee Reis believes that every recipe deserves the best and freshest ingredients bought daily from the market. "Since I put a lot of time into preparation and cooking," she says, "why risk inferior results?" She always buys foods in season and creates her menus accordingly—in other words, no tomato soup in December. She also enjoys mixing and matching textures and flavors to please the eye as well as the palate.

Her Menu 2 is ideal for a hot summer evening, with a cooling gazpacho topped with crabmeat as the first course. After the soup, she offers slices of turkey sausage—a blend of ground meat, minced wild mushrooms, and seasonings. A cream sauce flecked with tarragon is spooned over the sausage just before serving.

In Menu 1, a meal that could be served year-round, pan-fried noodles provide a crunchy base for the strips of turkey and vegetables in the salad. A piquant hot-and-sour salad dressing offsets the delicate flavors of the leek and mushroom soup.

Menu 3 presents moist slices of duck breast and turnips braised with diced onion—a rich and flavorful pairing. Chicory salad with tomato and shallots provides contrasting color and tartness to the main course.

A wedge of golden pan-fried noodles topped with shredded lettuce, vegetable strips, nuts, and turkey makes a colorful main course. For a buffet, serve the noodle pancake uncut on a round platter and mound the dressed salad on top. The clear broth is fragrant with leeks, mushrooms, and fresh ginger.

Leek and Mushroom Soup
Turkey Salad with Pan-Fried Noodles

For the noodle pancake, first soften the noodles by parboiling, then stir them with a long-pronged fork to break up any clumps before stir frying. The noodles will hold a pancake shape when fried because their surface starch causes them to stick together. Substitute fresh or dried spaghetti if Chinese egg noodles are unavailable.

WHAT TO DRINK

The cook recommends a slightly off-dry white wine such as a French Vouvray with this menu. A German *Kabinett*-class Riesling from the Rhine or Moselle area would also be good.

SHOPPING LIST AND STAPLES

2 to 3 pounds chicken backs, wings, necks, or other parts
1½-pound section of skinless, boneless turkey breast
8 medium-size fresh cultivated mushrooms (about ¼ pound total weight)
2 cucumbers
2 small red bell peppers
1 head romaine lettuce
2 small leeks (about ½ pound total weight)
1 bunch scallions
1-inch piece fresh ginger
2 cloves garlic
1 egg
1 cup chicken stock, preferably homemade (see page 11), or canned
½ pound fresh or dried thin Chinese egg noodles
1 cup vegetable oil, approximately
1 tablespoon Oriental sesame oil, approximately
1 tablespoon light Chinese soy sauce
2 tablespoons red wine vinegar
1 tablespoon peanut butter or sesame paste (tahini)
4-ounce can walnut pieces
1 tablespoon cornstarch
1 teaspoon sugar
½ teaspoon Cayenne pepper
¼ teaspoon dry mustard
Salt and freshly ground pepper
1 tablespoon dry sherry

UTENSILS

Food processor or blender
Stockpot

Large heavy-gauge skillet, preferably nonstick, with cover
Large saucepan
Medium-size heavy-gauge saucepan with cover
2 large bowls
Medium-size nonaluminum bowl
9-inch pie pan
Heatproof platter
Colander
Strainer
Measuring cups and spoons
Chef's knife
Paring knife
2 wooden spoons
Large spoon or mesh skimmer
Metal spatula
Grater (if not using processor)

START-TO-FINISH STEPS

1. Wash, dry, and prepare scallions for soup and salad recipes. Prepare ginger for soup and salad recipes.
2. Follow soup recipe steps 1 and 2.
3. While soup simmers, follow turkey recipe steps 1 through 6 and noodles recipe step 1.
4. Follow turkey recipe steps 7 and 8 and noodles recipe step 2.
5. While noodles are cooking, follow soup recipe step 3.
6. Follow noodles recipe steps 3 and 4 and soup recipe steps 4 through 8.
7. Follow noodles recipe steps 5 through 8.
8. Follow turkey recipe steps 9 through 11
9. Follow soup recipe step 9 and turkey recipe step 12, and serve.

RECIPES

Leek and Mushroom Soup

2 to 3 pounds chicken backs, wings, necks, or other parts
2 thin slices fresh ginger
2 whole scallions cut into 2-inch pieces, plus 2 thinly sliced scallion tops for garnish
2 small leeks (about ½ pound total weight)
8 medium-size fresh cultivated mushrooms (about ¼ pound total weight)
1 tablespoon vegetable oil
1 teaspoon salt

1. Prepare stock: In large saucepan combine chicken parts, ginger, and scallion pieces with 2 to 3 quarts cold water and bring to a boil over high heat. With large spoon or mesh skimmer, skim off foam, reduce heat, cover, and simmer, skimming occasionally, 40 minutes.

2. Meanwhile, trim off root ends of leeks and upper parts of leaves, and split leeks lengthwise. Gently spread leaves and rinse under cold running water to remove any sand and grit; dry with paper towel. Cut leeks into ⅛-inch-thick slices. Wipe mushrooms clean with damp paper towels. Cut into ¼-inch-thick slices.

3. Remove stock from heat and set aside to cool.

4. Heat oil in medium-size heavy-gauge saucepan over medium heat. Add leeks and sauté, stirring occasionally, 5 minutes, or until limp.

5. Pour stock through strainer set over large bowl.

6. Add mushrooms to leeks and sauté, stirring, 2 to 3 minutes.

7. Add 1 quart stock and salt to saucepan, and bring to a boil. Reduce heat and simmer 5 to 7 minutes, or until vegetables are just tender.

8. Cover pan, remove from heat, and keep warm.

9. When ready to serve, reheat soup if necessary, and divide soup among 4 bowls, and garnish with thinly sliced scallion tops.

Turkey Salad with Pan-Fried Noodles

1½-pound section of skinless, boneless turkey breast
1 egg
1 tablespoon dry sherry
1 teaspoon salt
1 tablespoon cornstarch
½ cup walnut pieces
2 cucumbers
2 small red bell peppers
1 head romaine lettuce
2 thinly sliced scallions

Dressing:
2 cloves garlic
1 teaspoon minced fresh ginger
¼ teaspoon dry mustard
½ teaspoon salt
½ teaspoon freshly ground pepper
1 teaspoon sugar
½ teaspoon Cayenne pepper
1 tablespoon light Chinese soy sauce
1 tablespoon peanut butter or sesame paste (tahini)
2 tablespoons red wine vinegar
1 teaspoon Oriental sesame oil
1 tablespoon vegetable oil
1 cup chicken stock

½ cup vegetable oil
Pan-Fried Noodles (see following recipe)

1. Preheat oven to 350 degrees.

2. With chef's knife, cut turkey breast against grain into strips 1½ inches long by ½ inch wide.

3. Separate egg, placing white in medium-size non-aluminum bowl and reserving yolk for another use. Add sherry, salt, and cornstarch to egg white and stir with fork until blended. Add turkey and toss until evenly coated; set aside to marinate at least 30 minutes.

4. Coarsely chop walnuts with chef's knife. Place walnuts in pie pan and toast in oven, shaking pan occasionally, 8 to 10 minutes, or until brown.

5. Meanwhile, peel, seed, and coarsely grate cucumbers. Wash, halve, core, and seed bell peppers. Cut peppers lengthwise into ¼-inch-wide strips.

6. Remove nuts from oven and set aside to cool. Reduce oven temperature to 200 degrees.

7. Wash lettuce and dry with paper towels; discard any bruised or discolored leaves. Stack leaves together and cut crosswise into ¼-inch-wide strips; set aside.

8. Peel and mince garlic for dressing. Combine with remaining dressing ingredients in food processor or blender and process until smooth.

9. Line plate with paper towels.

10. Heat ½ cup vegetable oil in large heavy-gauge skillet over medium-high heat until shimmering but not smoking. Carefully add turkey strips and fry, stirring occasionally, 3 to 4 minutes, or until crisp and golden brown. Transfer to paper-towel-lined plate to drain.

11. Return turkey to medium-size bowl and toss with about ½ cup dressing until evenly coated. Refrigerate remaining dressing in a tightly covered jar for another use.

12. Divide pan-fried noodles among 4 dinner plates. Top with layers of shredded lettuce, grated cucumber, red pepper strips, walnuts, sliced scallions, and turkey.

Pan-Fried Noodles

½ pound fresh or dried thin Chinese egg noodles
1½ teaspoons Oriental sesame oil
1 tablespoon salt
⅓ cup vegetable oil, approximately

1. Bring 2 quarts of water to a boil in stockpot over high heat.

2. Add noodles and cook 2 to 3 minutes for fresh, according to package directions for dried, or until *al dente*.

3. Transfer noodles to colander, rinse under cold running water, and drain. Gently pat dry with paper towels.

4. In large bowl, combine noodles with sesame oil and salt and toss until noodles are evenly coated with oil.

5. In large heavy-gauge skillet, heat ⅓ cup vegetable oil over medium-high heat until oil is hot enough to sizzle a piece of noodle. Reduce heat to medium and add noodles, swirling them to prevent sticking. With metal spatula, press noodles into pancake shape, cover skillet, and cook noodle pancake until bottom is golden, about 5 minutes.

6. With spatula, turn noodle pancake and fry another 3 to 4 minutes, drizzling an extra spoonful of oil around sides of pan, if necessary, to prevent sticking.

7. Line heatproof platter with paper towels.

8. Loosen sides of noodle pancake with spatula, transfer to platter, and keep warm in 200-degree oven.

Crabmeat Gazpacho
Turkey and Wild Mushroom Sausage with Tarragon Cream Sauce

Gazpacho garnished with crabmeat and scallions is a refreshing complement for slices of turkey sausage with tarragon cream sauce.

Gazpacho, often called liquid salad, is a refreshing hot-weather recipe that tastes best when vegetables are at their peak. Gazpacho usually includes chopped onion, tomato, green bell pepper, cucumber, and garlic in varying proportions, and is traditionally served with cubed tomato, bell pepper, and onion as garnish. For this version, the cook adds beef stock and liquid seasonings to the soup, and tops each serving with pieces of crabmeat and scallions. If you use frozen crabmeat instead of fresh, thaw it slowly, drain off excess liquid, and dry with paper towels before using.

Dried wild mushrooms, such as *cèpes*, *porcini*, or morels, are generally imported from Europe and are costly but worth the price—a few go a long way. Look for them in cellophane packets in specialty food stores. Dried mushrooms keep well for up to a year when stored in a cool place in a tightly closed container. Be sure to rinse these dried varieties well before use to remove as much grit as possible.

WHAT TO DRINK

A full-bodied white wine is essential here. A quality California Chardonnay from the Alexander Valley or Carneros area would be good, as would a white Montrachet Burgundy from Puligny or Chassagne.

1½-pound section of skinless boneless turkey breast
¼ pound fresh or frozen crabmeat
4 large ripe tomatoes (about 2½ pounds total weight)
2 cucumbers
2 carrots
Small bunch celery
¼ pound fresh cultivated mushrooms
Medium-size onion
Small bunch scallions (optional)
2 shallots
1 clove garlic
Small bunch fresh parsley
Small bunch fresh tarragon, or 1 teaspoon dried
1 lemon
1½ cups chicken stock, preferably homemade (see
   page 11), or canned
1 cup beef stock
2 eggs, 1 optional
½ pint light cream or half-and-half
½ pint heavy cream
1½ tablespoons unsalted butter
1 cup plus 3 tablespoons vegetable oil
2 tablespoons tarragon-flavored wine vinegar
2 tablespoons red wine vinegar
Dash of Worcestershire sauce
Dash of hot pepper sauce
1-ounce package dried porcini mushrooms, cèpes, or
   morels
¼ teaspoon dry mustard
¼ teaspoon Cayenne pepper
Salt and freshly ground black and white pepper
1 tablespoon brandy
2 tablespoons dry vermouth or dry white wine

UTENSILS

Food processor or blender
Medium-size skillet
Medium-size saucepan
Small saucepan
15 x 11-inch roasting pan
2 large bowls, 1 nonaluminum
2 small bowls
Colander
Strainer
Measuring cups and spoons
Chef's knife
Paring knife
Wooden spoon
Slotted spoon
Rubber spatula
Tongs
Melon baller or teaspoon
Vegetable peeler
Juicer
Cheesecloth

START-TO-FINISH STEPS

1. Prepare parsley, and fresh tarragon if using, for turkey and sauce recipes. Wash scallions, if using, trim and cut enough into 1-inch-long pieces to measure ¼ cup for gazpacho recipe.
2. Follow turkey recipe steps 1 through 4.
3. Follow gazpacho recipe steps 1 through 5.
4. Follow turkey recipe steps 5 through 10.
5. Follow sauce recipe steps 1 through 4.
6. Follow turkey recipe step 11.
7. Follow gazpacho recipe steps 6 and 7, turkey recipe step 12, and serve.

RECIPES

Crabmeat Gazpacho

Medium-size onion
1 clove garlic
4 large ripe tomatoes (about 2½ pounds total weight)
2 cucumbers
3 tablespoons vegetable oil
2 tablespoons red wine vinegar
1 cup beef stock
Salt and freshly ground black pepper
¼ teaspoon Cayenne pepper
Dash of hot pepper sauce
Dash of Worcestershire sauce
¼ pound fresh or frozen crabmeat
¼ cup sliced scallions for garnish (optional)

1. Bring 1 quart of water to a boil in medium-size saucepan over high heat.
2. Meanwhile, peel and coarsely chop onion and garlic.
3. Plunge tomatoes into boiling water and blanch 1 minute to loosen skins. With slotted spoon, transfer tomatoes to colander and refresh under cold running water. Peel, core, halve, and seed tomatoes; chop coarsely.
4. Peel cucumbers and halve lengthwise. Remove seeds with melon baller or teaspoon and discard. Chop coarsely.
5. Combine tomatoes, onion, garlic, cucumbers, oil, vinegar, stock, and seasoning to taste in food processor or blender and purée coarsely. Adjust seasoning, if necessary. Transfer gazpacho to large nonaluminum bowl, cover with plastic wrap, and refrigerate until ready to serve. Rinse processor or blender container.
6. Flake crabmeat to measure ½ cup and place in small bowl. Remove and discard any shell or cartilage.
7. When ready to serve, divide gazpacho among 4 soup bowls and garnish each serving with 2 tablespoons crabmeat, and some sliced scallions, if desired.

Turkey and Wild Mushroom Sausage with Tarragon Cream Sauce

1-ounce package dried porcini mushrooms, cèpes, or
   morels
1½ cups chicken stock

1½-pound section of skinless, boneless turkey breast
1 egg (optional)
¼ pound fresh cultivated mushrooms
2 stalks celery
2 carrots
2 shallots
1½ tablespoons unsalted butter
1 tablespoon chopped parsley
Salt and freshly ground white pepper
1 cup heavy cream
1 tablespoon brandy
Tarragon Cream Sauce (see following recipe)

1. Place container of food processor or blender in freezer to chill.
2. Rinse dried mushrooms under cold running water. Combine mushrooms and stock in small saucepan and bring to a boil over medium-high heat. Simmer uncovered 20 minutes, or until stock is reduced by half.
3. Rinse turkey and dry with paper towels; cut into 1½-inch cubes. In chilled bowl of food processor or blender, process turkey about 1 minute, or until it is smooth and not runny. If it doesn't hold together, separate egg, add white to turkey, one half at a time, and process until incorporated. Reserve yolk for another use. Transfer puréed turkey to large bowl, cover, and chill in freezer 10 to 15 minutes. Rinse processor or blender container.
4. Wipe fresh mushrooms clean with damp paper towels. Wash celery and carrots, and dry with paper towels. Trim celery; peel and trim carrots. Using food processor or chef's knife, chop enough mushrooms, celery, and carrots to measure ¼ cup each. Peel and mince shallots.
5. Remove porcini mushrooms and stock from heat. Pour stock through damp cheesecloth-lined strainer set over small bowl, reserving mushrooms. Return stock to pan, bring to a boil over high heat, and continue to boil 6 to 8 minutes, or until syrupy and reduced to 1 to 2 tablespoons.
6. Meanwhile, heat butter in medium-size skillet over medium heat until foamy. Add shallots and sauté 1 minute. Add chopped vegetables and sauté, stirring occasionally, 3 minutes. Stir in parsley and season mixture with salt and pepper to taste; set aside.
7. Remove mushroom glaze from heat and set aside. Coarsely chop reserved porcini mushrooms and add to vegetable mixture.
8. Return chilled turkey to bowl of processor or blender and, while machine is running, slowly add cream. Add brandy and mushroom glaze, and process just until combined. Adjust seasonings. Return turkey mixture to large bowl and fold in sautéed vegetables.
9. Place two 9 x 13-inch sheets of plastic wrap on work surface and lightly coat with oil. Divide turkey mixture between the 2 sheets and, with a wet rubber spatula, shape turkey mixture into 2 cylinders, each about 10 inches long and 1½ inches in diameter. Enclose each sausage tightly in plastic wrap; there should be no air holes. Using 2 more sheets of plastic for each sausage, roll lengthwise and then widthwise to make watertight.
10. Fill roasting pan half full of water and bring to a

simmer over medium heat. Add sausages, making sure water covers them, and poach, turning at least once, about 20 minutes, or until firm.
11. Remove pan from heat and allow sausages to cool in the water until ready to serve. Sausages should be served warm or at room temperature, not hot.
12. When ready to serve, unwrap sausages and cut into ½-inch-thick slices. Divide slices among 4 dinner plates and top with tarragon cream sauce.

Tarragon Cream Sauce

1 lemon
1 egg
½ teaspoon salt
¼ teaspoon freshly ground white pepper
¼ teaspoon dry mustard
2 tablespoons tarragon-flavored wine vinegar
1 tablespoon chopped fresh tarragon, or 1 teaspoon dried
1 tablespoon chopped fresh parsley
1 cup vegetable oil
¼ cup light cream or half-and-half
2 tablespoons dry vermouth or dry white wine

1. Squeeze enough lemon juice to measure 1 teaspoon.
2. In food processor or blender, combine egg, salt, pepper, dry mustard, lemon juice, wine vinegar, fresh or dried tarragon, and fresh parsley, and process until combined.
3. With machine running, slowly add oil and process until sauce is very thick and smooth.
4. With machine running, add light cream and dry vermouth, and process until blended. Adjust seasoning and set aside until ready to serve.

ADDED TOUCH

The glaze for these braised carrots is not cloyingly sweet. Chives provide contrasting color and flavor.

Braised Carrots with Fresh Chives

1 pound carrots
1 tablespoon unsalted butter
1 teaspoon sugar
½ teaspoon salt
¼ teaspoon freshly ground white pepper
Large bunch fresh chives

1. Preheat oven to 200 degrees.
2. Peel carrots and cut on diagonal into 2-inch-long pieces.
3. Combine carrots, butter, sugar, salt, pepper, and 1 cup water in skillet and bring to a boil over high heat. Reduce to a simmer, cover pan, and cook 4 minutes.
4. Place heatproof bowl in oven to warm.
5. Meanwhile, wash fresh chives and dry with paper towels. Snip enough chives to measure ¼ cup; set aside.
6. With slotted spoon, transfer carrots to warm bowl. Return skillet to high heat and bring cooking liquid to a boil. Continue to boil 3 to 4 minutes, or until syrupy.
7. Pour syrup over carrots and toss until evenly coated. Sprinkle with chives and serve.

Chicory Salad with Tomato and Shallots
Duck with Port Wine and Caper Sauce
Braised Turnips and Onions

For company, serve chicory salad, slices of duck breast in a port wine and caper sauce, and a bowl of braised turnips with onions.

Holly Garrison

L ike many innovative cooks, Holly Garrison draws upon a lifetime of food memories and practical experience when she puts together a meal. The cooking of Lancaster County in the Pennsylvania German country where she grew up often influences her menus, and she learned long ago that meals need not be time consuming to be good.

According to Holly Garrison, "The Pennsylvania Germans never skimp when it comes to cooking good food, and they make frequent use of such exotic spices as saffron." In Menu 1, the pot pie (or *botboi* in the Pennsylvania German dialect) contains saffron for color and flavor. It differs from standard pot pies because the cook uses egg noodles rather than a pastry crust. With the pot pie, she offers a sweet-and-sour cucumber and onion salad.

Menu 2 presents Turkey Pojarski, a dish reputedly named for the Polish innkeeper who invented it. Any meat or fish prepared *à la Pojarski* is minced, seasoned, and then reshaped into a new form before being cooked. In this version, ground turkey breast is blended with *crème fraîche*, then shaped into patties, which are sautéed briefly and topped with apple slices and prunes.

Holly Garrison's Menu 3 proves that preparing duck can be quick *and* economical: One bird easily serves four when it is cut into individual pieces and covered with a rich, creamy wine sauce. A spinach salad sprinkled with duck-skin cracklings and wild rice with pecans are the ample side dishes.

The turkey pot pie with egg noodles can be served in individual gratin dishes or in one large, deep platter. Crescents of cucumber and thin slices of red onion in a sweet-and-sour dressing are a tangy contrast to the main dish.

57

Pennsylvania German Turkey Pot Pie
Sweet-and-Sour Cucumber and Red Onion Salad

Turkey pot pie is a hearty meat-and-pastry dish that can vary according to the season, the cook's whim, and what is in the larder. This Pennsylvania German recipe uses all dark meat, which you can purchase precooked at a supermarket or butcher, or prepare yourself if you have extra time (see Turkey Stock recipe, page 59). Here the turkey is combined with homemade egg noodles.

Roll out and cut the noodles, then allow them to dry uncovered for several minutes to firm up before cooking. If you do not plan to use the noodles right away, cover them with plastic wrap. The noodles cook in the turkey stock and absorb its flavors as they become tender.

A sweet-and-sour dish is traditionally a part of every Pennsylvania German meal. Here it is a salad of cucumber and onion slices in a milk and vinegar dressing.

WHAT TO DRINK

An uncomplicated white wine would go well with this menu. Try a Soave from Italy or a Sylvaner from Alsace.

SHOPPING LIST AND STAPLES

2 pounds cooked turkey dark meat, or 3 pounds turkey
    leg and thigh pieces (if making Turkey Stock)
Small head Bibb lettuce
2 medium-size cucumbers (about 1½ pounds total weight)
2 medium-size potatoes (about 1 pound total weight)
2 medium-size carrots (about ½ pound total weight)
Small bunch celery with leaves
Large yellow onion (if making Turkey Stock)
Medium-size red onion
Small bunch parsley
2 eggs
½ cup milk
6 tablespoons unsalted butter
4 cups chicken stock, preferably homemade (see page 11),
    or two 13¾-ounce cans (if not making Turkey Stock)
3 tablespoons white vinegar
1¾ cups all-purpose flour, approximately
1 teaspoon sugar
½ teaspoon ground sage
2 small bay leaves (if making Turkey Stock)
Pinch of saffron
Salt
5 or 6 peppercorns (if making Turkey Stock)
Freshly ground pepper

UTENSILS

Dutch oven with tight-fitting cover
17 x 11-inch baking sheet
1 large bowl, plus 1 additional if making Turkey Stock
2 medium-size bowls, plus 1 additional if making Turkey
    Stock
3 small bowls
Salad spinner (optional)
Colander
Large sieve (if making Turkey Stock)
Measuring cups and spoons
Chef's knife
Paring knife
Wooden spoon
Melon baller (optional)
Metal tongs (if making Turkey Stock)
Pastry cutter
Rolling pin

START-TO-FINISH STEPS

At least 1 hour ahead: If making homemade turkey stock, follow turkey stock recipe steps 1 through 3.

1. Follow salad recipe steps 1 through 3.
2. Follow turkey stock recipe step 4.
3. While stock is reducing, follow pot pie recipe steps 1 through 4.
4. Follow turkey stock recipe step 5.
5. Follow pot pie recipe step 5 and turkey stock recipe steps 6 and 7.
6. Follow pot pie recipe steps 6 through 9.
7. While pot pie is gently boiling, follow salad recipe steps 4 and 5.
8. Follow pot pie recipe step 10 and salad recipe step 6.
9. Follow pot pie recipe step 11 and serve with salad.

RECIPES

Pennsylvania German Turkey Pot Pie

6 tablespoons unsalted butter
2 medium-size potatoes (about 1 pound total weight)
2 medium-size carrots (about ½ pound total weight)
2 stalks celery
Small bunch parsley for garnish (optional)
1¾ cups all-purpose flour, approximately

Salt
2 eggs
4 cups chicken stock or Turkey Stock (see following recipe)
Pinch of saffron (if using chicken stock)
½ teaspoon ground sage
2 pounds cooked turkey dark meat
Freshly ground pepper

1. Set out butter to reach room temperature. Peel potatoes and cut into 1-inch dice to measure about 2 cups. Place potatoes in medium-size bowl and cover with cold water to prevent discoloration; set aside.
2. Peel carrots and cut crosswise into ¼-inch-thick slices to measure about 1 cup. Set carrots aside in small bowl.
3. Wash and trim celery. Cut crosswise into ¼-inch-thick slices to measure about 1 cup. Add celery to carrots.
4. Wash parsley, if using, and dry with paper towels. Chop enough to measure 2 tablespoons; set aside.
5. Combine 1¼ cups flour and ¼ teaspoon salt in medium-size bowl. Make a well in center of flour and crack eggs into it. Using your fingers or a fork, work eggs into dry ingredients until blended. Gather dough into a ball. Place dough on lightly floured work surface and knead for about 10 minutes.
6. Pour chicken stock or turkey stock into Dutch oven. If using chicken stock, add saffron. Over medium-low heat, bring stock to a slow boil.
7. Meanwhile, to make noodles: Divide dough in half. On generously floured surface, roll out one-half of dough as thinly as possible (you should be able to see the shadow of your fingers through it). This may take a few minutes, since this dough is particularly elastic and you may have to re-flour the surface a couple of times to keep the dough from sticking. Trim dough with a pastry cutter to make a rectangle. Cut rectangle into 1-inch squares, transferring squares to baking sheet as you cut them. Repeat with remaining dough.
8. Using fork, blend 6 tablespoons flour with an equal amount of butter in small bowl; add gradually to stock, stirring, until stock is desired thickness (you may not want to add all of flour-butter mixture).
9. Drain potatoes and add to stock along with carrots, celery, sage, and noodle squares, adjusting heat, if necessary, to keep stock at a slow boil. Boil gently, uncovered, 10 to 15 minutes, or until vegetables are tender and noodles are cooked.
10. Cut turkey meat into 1-inch pieces to measure about 4 cups. Stir turkey meat into stock and continue to simmer 2 to 3 minutes, or until heated through. Season with salt and pepper to taste.
11. Divide pot pie among 4 individual gratin dishes or deep plates and garnish with parsley, if desired.

Turkey Stock

Large yellow onion
Tops of 4 celery stalks
4 sprigs parsley
3 pounds turkey leg and thigh pieces
5 or 6 peppercorns
2 small bay leaves
Pinch of saffron

1. Peel onion and cut into thin wedges. Rinse celery tops and parsley sprigs.
2. Rinse turkey pieces under cold running water and place in Dutch oven. Add onion, celery tops, parsley, peppercorns, bay leaves, saffron, and enough cold water to cover, and bring to a slow boil over high heat. Reduce heat to medium-low, cover, and simmer gently about 1 hour, or until turkey is tender but not falling off the bones. The exact time will depend on the size of the turkey parts.
3. Using tongs, transfer turkey pieces to large bowl and cover loosely with foil.
4. Raise heat to high and bring stock to a rolling boil. Continue to boil, uncovered, about 15 minutes, or until liquid is reduced to about 4 cups.
5. Remove stock from heat and cool slightly.
6. Pour stock through large sieve set over medium-size bowl, pressing solids with back of wooden spoon to extract as much liquid as possible. Set stock aside for use in pot pie or other recipe as directed.
7. Pull skin off turkey pieces and discard; pull meat off bones in large chunks; discard bones and gristle. Cut turkey meat into 1-inch pieces to measure about 4 cups. Set meat aside for use in pot pie or other recipe as directed.

Sweet-and-Sour Cucumber and Red Onion Salad

2 medium-size cucumbers (about 1½ pounds total weight)
1 teaspoon salt
Medium-size red onion
½ cup milk
3 tablespoons white vinegar
1 teaspoon sugar
Small head Bibb lettuce

1. Peel cucumbers and halve lengthwise. Scoop out seeds with melon baller or teaspoon. Cut cucumber halves into ¼-inch-thick crescents and place in colander. Sprinkle cucumber crescents with ½ teaspoon salt and toss until evenly coated; set aside to drain.
2. Peel and halve onion lengthwise. Cut halves crosswise into ⅛-inch-thick slices; set aside.
3. In small bowl, combine milk, vinegar, sugar, and remaining salt, and stir until blended; set aside.
4. Wash lettuce and dry in salad spinner or with paper towels. Remove any bruised or discolored leaves and discard.
5. Combine cucumbers and onion in large bowl. Stir dressing to recombine, add dressing to bowl, and toss vegetables until evenly coated. If desired, pour off excess dressing.
6. Divide lettuce leaves among 4 plates and top with cucumbers and onion.

Turkey Pojarski with Sautéed Apple Slices
and Prunes in Port
Wilted Watercress

This company meal features turkey patties topped with prunes and fried apple circles, and wilted watercress on the side.

Crème fraîche, a principal ingredient in the turkey patties, is a cultured cream product with a slightly acidic taste. *Crème fraîche* is costly and often hard to find; you can use heavy cream, whipped just until it forms soft peaks, as a substitute.

WHAT TO DRINK

A delicate white wine, such as a Washington or New York State Riesling, or any *Kabinett*-class German Riesling from the Moselle region, would be good here.

SHOPPING LIST AND STAPLES

1¾-pound section of turkey breast, or 1¾ pounds
　ground turkey breast
3 bunches watercress
4 medium-size Golden Delicious or Rome Beauty apples
2 lemons
2 eggs
½ cup milk
⅔ cup crème fraîche

1 stick plus 4 tablespoons unsalted butter
¼ cup vegetable oil
6 slices firm white bread
¾ cup dry bread crumbs, approximately
1-pound package pitted prunes
1 stick cinnamon
Salt and freshly ground pepper
¼ cup ruby port

UTENSILS

Food processor, blender, or meat grinder
Large stockpot
Large skillet
Small nonaluminum saucepan with tight-fitting cover
Small heavy-gauge saucepan or butter warmer
Heatproof platter
Large bowl
Medium-size heatproof bowl
Small bowl
Colander
Measuring cups and spoons

Chef's knife
Boning knife
Paring knife
Wooden spoon
Metal spatula
Zester or grater
Metal tongs
Apple corer

START-TO-FINISH STEPS

Fifteen minutes ahead: In small saucepan or butter warmer, clarify butter (see page 10) for turkey recipe.

1. Follow prunes recipe steps 1 through 3.
2. Follow turkey recipe steps 1 through 4.
3. Follow watercress recipe steps 1 through 4 and apples recipe steps 1 and 2.
4. Follow turkey recipe steps 5 and 6.
5. Follow watercress recipe steps 5 through 7.
6. Follow turkey recipe step 7 and serve with watercress.

RECIPES

Turkey Pojarski with Sautéed Apple Slices and Prunes in Port

6 slices firm white bread
½ cup milk
1¾-pound section of turkey breast or 1¾ pounds ground turkey breast, chilled
6 tablespoons unsalted clarified butter
1 teaspoon salt
¼ teaspoon freshly ground pepper
⅔ cup crème fraîche
2 eggs
¾ cup dry bread crumbs, approximately
¼ cup vegetable oil
Sautéed Apple Slices (see following recipe)
Prunes in Port (see following recipe)

1. Preheat oven to 200 degrees.
2. Remove crusts from bread and discard. Tear bread into small pieces to measure about 3 cups and place in small bowl with milk to soak.
3. If using section of turkey breast, rinse and dry. With boning knife, remove skin and excess fat. Cut meat away from rib cage. Reserve skin and bones for stock. Cut turkey into large chunks and grind coarsely in food processor, in blender, or with meat grinder. You will have about 4 cups ground meat. Turn ground turkey into large bowl.
4. Squeeze excess milk from bread and add to turkey with 2 tablespoons clarified butter, salt, pepper, and crème fraîche. Separate eggs, adding yolks to turkey mixture; reserve whites for another use. Knead mixture with hands until thoroughly blended. Cover turkey with plastic wrap and place in freezer to chill for at least 10 minutes.
5. Place bread crumbs on sheet of waxed paper. Remove bowl from freezer and shape mixture into 8 patties, each about ½-inch thick; taper patties slightly at one end to resemble chops. Dip each patty into bread crumbs.
6. Heat remaining clarified butter and oil in large skillet over medium-high heat. When butter stops foaming, add as many patties as will fit in pan without crowding. Lower heat to medium and sauté 2½ to 3 minutes per side, or until firm and lightly browned. Transfer to heatproof platter and keep warm in oven. Repeat for remaining patties.
7. Divide patties among 4 dinner plates and serve topped with sautéed apple slices and prunes in port.

Sautéed Apple Slices

4 medium-size Golden Delicious or Rome Beauty apples
4 tablespoons unsalted butter

1. Rinse, dry, and core apples. Cut ⅛-inch-thick slice from each end of apples and discard. Cut each apple crosswise into ½-inch-thick rounds.
2. Heat half the butter in large skillet over medium-high heat. Add half the apple slices and sauté about 2½ minutes per side, or until lightly browned. Transfer apple slices to heatproof platter and keep warm in 200-degree oven until ready to serve. Repeat process for remaining apples.

Prunes in Port

1 lemon
¼ cup ruby port
1 stick cinnamon
1 cup (about 18) pitted prunes

1. Rinse and dry lemon. Using zester or grater, remove enough rind to measure 1 teaspoon.
2. Combine lemon rind, port, cinnamon stick, and ¼ cup water in small nonaluminum saucepan and bring to a boil over high heat. Reduce heat to medium-low and simmer mixture gently, covered, 5 minutes.
3. Remove pan from heat. Stir in prunes, cover, and set aside, stirring occasionally, at least 10 minutes or until ready to serve.

Wilted Watercress

Salt
2 tablespoons unsalted butter
1 lemon
3 bunches watercress
Freshly ground pepper

1. Bring 4 quarts of lightly salted water to a boil in large stockpot over high heat. Melt butter in small heavy-gauge saucepan over low heat; set aside.
2. Place medium-size heatproof serving bowl in 200-degree oven to warm.
3. Squeeze enough lemon juice to measure ½ tablespoon.
4. Wash watercress; trim off stems and discard.
5. Stirring constantly with wooden spoon, drop watercress by handfuls into the rapidly boiling water.
6. Immediately transfer watercress to colander and drain. Turn into warm bowl.
7. Add melted butter, lemon juice, and salt and pepper to taste to watercress and toss to combine.

Danièle Delpeuch

MENU 1 (Right)
Turkey with Prunes and Cream Sauce
Tomato Tart
Chicory Salad with Lardons

MENU 2
Turkey Paupiettes
Sautéed Broccoli
Lentils Vinaigrette

MENU 3
Braised Duck with Onions
Zucchini Flan
Belgian Endive and Orange Salad

A devotee of the rich, hearty cooking of Périgord, Danièle Delpeuch has dedicated a great deal of her time to learning the traditional culinary methods of that region. Primarily agricultural, Périgord offers an abundance of fresh produce and superb poultry, and cooks regularly shop the farmers' markets for the best buys. For her three menus, Danièle Delpeuch selects dishes typical of southwestern France and adapts them for the American kitchen.

The entrée of Menu 1 is based on a dish popular in the Dordogne River valley, where most well-equipped farm kitchens have a prune-drying oven. Instead of serving the usual rabbit with prunes, however, the cook substitutes boneless turkey breast, which goes equally well with the fruit. A mustardy tomato tart and a salad of chicory with *lardons* (coarsely diced bacon) are the accompaniments.

For Menu 2, she offers a Périgourdine dish traditionally served at wedding banquets and known locally as *oiseaux sans têtes*, or birds without heads. The bird here is turkey—in the form of scallops—rolled around a seasoned mixture of mushrooms, Smithfield ham, and chicken livers. In Périgord a cook would use wild *cèpes*, Bayonne ham, and *foie gras*—and add sliced truffles to the sauce just before serving.

Usually, when preparing a duck recipe at home, this cook uses her own farm-raised Barbarie ducklings. Menu 3 is her adaptation of a simple regional specialty—whole braised duckling with onions. Here the duck is quartered and its juices combine with sweet onions as the seasoning for the meat. With this hearty main dish, she serves zucchini flan and a light bittersweet salad of Belgian endive and orange sections.

An ample portion of turkey with plump prunes and cream sauce, chicory salad with lardons, *and a wedge of tomato tart make a substantial meal for family or company.*

64

Turkey with Prunes and Cream Sauce
Tomato Tart
Chicory Salad with Lardons

To make a successful tart crust by hand, use the same amounts of ingredients given for the food processor method (page 67), but make sure the butter is cool yet pliable. Gently mix the egg yolk with the butter before adding it to the flour and baking powder (to assure even distribution). Add just enough ice water to make the ingredients cohere when blended with your fingers or with a pastry blender. When rolling out the dough, handle it gently and quickly; otherwise the butter will soften and the pastry will be tough and greasy.

WHAT TO DRINK

Select an Alsatian Pinot Blanc or a Gewürztraminer for this menu. Or try the same wines from Italy or California.

SHOPPING LIST AND STAPLES

1-pound section of boneless, skinless turkey breast
¼ pound slab bacon (4 to 5 slices)
Large head chicory
Small bunch fresh parsley
1 lemon
16-ounce can Italian plum tomatoes
1 cup duck stock or chicken stock, preferably homemade
    (see page 11), or canned
3 large eggs
½ pint heavy cream
1 stick plus 1 tablespoon unsalted butter, approximately
2 ounces Gruyère cheese
3 tablespoons duck fat (see page 9) or chicken fat
1 tablespoon vegetable oil, plus 3 tablespoons (if not using
    duck fat or chicken fat)
2 tablespoons Dijon mustard
8-ounce package pitted whole prunes
1⅔ cups all-purpose flour
½ teaspoon baking powder
1 teaspoon saffron threads
Salt and freshly ground pepper

UTENSILS

Food processor (optional)
2 large heavy-gauge skillets
8-inch quiche or tart pan
Medium-size bowl, plus 1 additional (if not using
    processor)
2 small bowls
Strainer
Measuring cups and spoons
Chef's knife
Paring knife
2 wooden spoons
Whisk
Slotted spoon
Grater (if not using processor)
Rolling pin
Pastry blender (if not using processor)
Pastry brush

START-TO-FINISH STEPS

1. Wash parsley and dry with paper towels. Chop parsley to measure 2 tablespoons for turkey recipe and 1 tablespoon for salad recipe.
2. Follow turkey recipe step 1 and salad recipe step 1.
3. Follow tomato tart recipe steps 1 through 8.
4. While the tomato tart is baking, follow turkey recipe steps 2 and 3.
5. Follow turkey recipe step 4 and salad recipe steps 2 through 6.
6. Follow tomato tart recipe step 9, turkey recipe step 5, and serve with salad.

RECIPES

Turkey with Prunes and Cream Sauce

1 cup pitted whole prunes
1-pound section of boneless, skinless turkey breast
3 tablespoons duck fat, chicken fat, or vegetable oil
Salt and freshly ground pepper
1 cup duck stock or chicken stock
½ cup heavy cream
1 teaspoon saffron threads
2 tablespoons chopped fresh parsley

1. In small bowl, combine prunes with enough warm water to cover and let soak 15 minutes.
2. Rinse turkey and dry with paper towels. Cut in half horizontally, then cut into 2-inch-long, ¼-inch-thick strips.
3. In large heavy-gauge skillet, heat fat or oil over medium heat. Add turkey strips, season with salt and pepper, and sauté, stirring occasionally, about 5 minutes, or until lightly browned on all sides.
4. Add stock, reduce heat to medium, and simmer about

15 minutes, uncovered, or until reduced to about ½ cup.

5. Drain prunes and add to skillet. Stir in cream, saffron, and parsley, and simmer just until heated through. Divide among 4 dinner plates and serve immediately.

Tomato Tart

Pastry:
1 stick unsalted butter, chilled, plus 1 tablespoon for greasing pan
1⅔ cups all-purpose flour
½ teaspoon baking powder
Large egg
Pinch of salt

Filling:
16-ounce can Italian plum tomatoes
2 ounces Gruyère cheese
2 tablespoons Dijon mustard
2 large eggs
½ cup heavy cream
Salt and freshly ground pepper

1. Preheat oven to 350 degrees. Butter 8-inch quiche or tart pan and set aside.

2. For pastry: Cut 1 stick butter into pieces. Combine flour and baking powder in food processor fitted with steel blade and process briefly to blend. Separate egg, adding yolk to dry ingredients in processor and reserving white for another use. Add butter, salt, and 1 tablespoon ice water, and process, adding more ice water, 1 tablespoon at a time, just until dough gathers around blade, 10 to 15 seconds. Or see page 66 for hand method.

3. On lightly floured surface, roll out pastry into a 10-inch round and fit into prepared pan. Trim off excess pastry and flute edge. Rinse and dry processor bowl, if using.

4. For filling: Turn tomatoes into strainer set over medium-size bowl and drain; reserve juice for another use. Quarter tomatoes.

5. Grate enough Gruyère to measure ¼ cup.

6. Brush bottom of pastry shell with mustard. Arrange tomatoes in shell and press down gently with fork.

7. In small bowl, combine 2 eggs, cream, and salt and pepper to taste, and whisk until blended. Pour egg mixture over tomatoes and sprinkle with Gruyère.

8. Bake tart in center of oven 30 minutes, or until pastry is golden and tart is set in middle.

9. Cut tart into generous wedges and divide among 4 small plates.

Chicory Salad with Lardons

Large head chicory
¼ pound slab bacon (4 to 5 slices)
1 tablespoon vegetable oil
1 lemon
1 tablespoon chopped fresh parsley
Salt and freshly ground pepper

1. Wash chicory and dry with paper towels. Remove any bruised or discolored leaves and discard. Break into bite-size pieces and place in salad bowl. Cover and refrigerate until ready to serve.

2. Line plate with paper towels.

3. In large heavy-gauge skillet, bring about 1 inch of water to a rapid boil over high heat. While water is heating, cut bacon into ¾-inch cubes. Add bacon to boiling water and blanch about 2 minutes, or until softened. With slotted spoon, transfer bacon to towel-lined plate; rinse skillet and dry.

4. Add oil to skillet and heat over medium-high heat 30 seconds. Add bacon and sauté, stirring occasionally, until browned and crisp, about 5 minutes.

5. Meanwhile, halve lemon and juice one half; reserve remaining half for another use.

6. Remove chicory from refrigerator. Add warm bacon and fat from pan to chicory, sprinkle with lemon juice and parsley, and season with salt and pepper to taste. Toss salad to combine, and divide among dinner plates.

ADDED TOUCH

Be sure to have the egg whites at room temperature before beating them, and make sure beater and bowl are grease free or the whites will not expand properly.

Walnut Mousse

1 cup walnut pieces
2 large eggs
1 cup milk
¼ cup sugar
2 tablespoons all-purpose flour
4 ounces (4 squares) semisweet chocolate
6 tablespoons unsalted butter

1. Finely grind walnuts.

2. Separate eggs, placing yolks in small bowl and whites in medium-size bowl.

3. In small saucepan, bring milk just to a boil over medium heat. Meanwhile, add sugar and flour to egg yolks and whisk until well blended. Whisk a little of the hot milk into egg yolk mixture and then add yolk mixture to milk in saucepan, whisking until blended.

4. Bring mixture to a boil over medium heat, whisking constantly.

5. Remove pan from heat and fold in walnuts.

6. In medium-size bowl, beat egg whites with electric mixer at high speed until stiff. Fold one-third of egg whites into mousse and then gently fold mousse into remaining egg white.

7. With rubber spatula, turn mousse into a deep serving dish. If serving immediately, set aside at room temperature; or cover and refrigerate until ready to serve.

8. Just before serving, combine chocolate and butter in top half of double boiler over, not in, barely simmering water, and heat, stirring occasionally with metal spoon, until chocolate is melted.

9. Divide mousse among individual bowls and top each serving with hot chocolate sauce.

Turkey Paupiettes
Sautéed Broccoli
Lentils Vinaigrette

A flavorful ham, such as Smithfield or prosciutto, is used in the stuffing for the turkey scallops. Smithfield is the name of a special type of dry-cured, smoked, and aged ham processed only in Smithfield, Virginia. The most famous of all American country hams, a Smithfield has salty, dark red meat. It can be purchased at a butcher or gourmet shop or through the mail. Prosciutto is an Italian-style dry-cured unsmoked ham; its moist deep pink meat is well seasoned but not particularly salty. Prosciutto is sold at Italian groceries and specialty food stores.

Impress your guests with a French country dinner: thin turkey scallops wrapped around a savory filling, sautéed broccoli florets, and lentils vinaigrette garnished with diced red peppers and parsley.

WHAT TO DRINK

This meal demands a balanced and subtle red wine. Try a Bordeaux from one of the less expensive classified growths, a moderately priced California Merlot, or a Cabernet from northern Italy.

SHOPPING LIST AND STAPLES

1-pound section of boneless, skinless turkey breast, cut into four ¼-inch-thick scallops
¼ pound Smithfield ham, prosciutto, or other dry-cured ham, unsliced
2 ounces chicken livers (about 2 livers)
½ pound fresh cultivated white mushrooms
1 head broccoli

Medium-size onion
Medium-size carrot
Small red bell pepper
3 cloves garlic
3 shallots
Large bunch fresh parsley
Small bunch fresh thyme, or ½ teaspoon dried
2 large eggs
½ pint crème fraîche or heavy cream
3 tablespoons vegetable oil, plus 5 tablespoons (if not
    using duck fat)
5 tablespoons duck fat, see page 9 (optional)
1½ tablespoons white wine vinegar
½ pound brown lentils (about 1 cup)
1 bay leaf
Salt
Freshly ground pepper
⅓ cup Madeira wine
⅓ cup dry white wine

UTENSILS

Food processor (optional)
2 large heavy-gauge skillets
Large saucepan
Heatproof platter
Large bowl

Medium-size heatproof bowl, plus 1 additional bowl (if not
    using processor)
Small bowl
Colander
Strainer
Measuring cups and spoons
Meat pounder or cleaver
Chef's knife
Paring knife
2 wooden spoons
Metal tongs
Cheesecloth
Kitchen string

START-TO-FINISH STEPS

1. Peel and finely chop shallots and 1 garlic clove for lentils recipe. Peel and coarsely chop remaining 2 cloves garlic for turkey recipe. Wash parsley, and fresh thyme if using, and dry with paper towels. Finely mince enough parsley to measure 3 tablespoons for turkey recipe and chop enough to measure 2 tablespoons for lentils recipe.

2. Follow lentils recipe steps 1 through 4.

3. While lentils simmer, follow turkey recipe steps 1 through 7.

4. While turkey is browning, follow lentils recipe steps 5 and 6.

5. Follow turkey recipe steps 8 through 10.
6. While sauce is reducing, follow broccoli recipe steps 1 through 4.
7. Follow turkey recipe steps 11 and 12, and lentils recipe steps 7 and 8.
8. Follow turkey recipe step 13 and serve with broccoli and lentils.

RECIPES

Turkey Paupiettes

1-pound section of boneless, skinless turkey breast, cut into four ¼-inch-thick scallops
Salt and freshly ground pepper
¼ pound Smithfield ham, prosciutto, or other dry-cured ham, unsliced
2 ounces chicken livers (about 2 livers)
½ pound fresh cultivated white mushrooms
2 cloves garlic, coarsely chopped
3 tablespoons finely minced parsley
2 large eggs
3 tablespoons duck fat (see page 9) or vegetable oil
⅓ cup Madeira wine
⅓ cup dry white wine
¾ cup crème fraîche or heavy cream

1. Place each turkey scallop between two sheets of waxed paper and gently pound with meat pounder or cleaver to about ⅛-inch thickness. Season scallops on both sides with salt and pepper.
2. Trim off excess fat from ham and discard. Rinse chicken livers under cold running water and dry with paper towels. Remove membranes and discard. Coarsely chop ham to make about ¾ cup and chop chicken livers.
3. Wipe mushrooms clean with damp paper towels and chop coarsely to measure about 2½ cups.
4. In food processor fitted with steel blade, combine ham, chicken livers, mushrooms, garlic, and 1 tablespoon parsley. Separate eggs, adding yolks to processor and reserving whites for another use, and process until mixture is well combined, about 20 seconds. Or, mince ingredients with chef's knife and combine with yolks in medium-size bowl.
5. Spread about 2 tablespoons of stuffing mixture on each flattened turkey scallop. Roll up scallops, tucking in edges, and tie securely with kitchen string. Reserve remaining stuffing mixture.
6. Preheat oven to 200 degrees.
7. In large heavy-gauge skillet, heat duck fat or oil over medium heat. Add the paupiettes and sauté, turning occasionally, about 10 minutes, or until lightly browned.
8. Transfer paupiettes to heatproof platter and keep warm in oven.
9. Add remaining stuffing to skillet and sauté, stirring, 1 minute. Stir in Madeira and white wine, and bring to a boil over medium-high heat, scraping up any brown bits clinging to bottom of pan. Return paupiettes and any accumulated juices to skillet and cook, turning occasionally, 8 to 12 minutes, or until sauce is syrupy and reduced by half.

10. Meanwhile, place 4 dinner plates in oven to warm.
11. Using tongs, transfer paupiettes to warmed dinner plates and remove strings.
12. Stir crème fraîche or heavy cream into sauce and simmer 1 to 2 minutes, or until heated through. Add salt and pepper to taste.
13. Spoon sauce over each paupiette and sprinkle with remaining parsley.

Sautéed Broccoli

1 head broccoli
2 tablespoons duck fat or vegetable oil
Salt and freshly ground pepper

1. Wash and trim broccoli; cut into large florets.
2. In large heavy-gauge skillet, heat duck fat or oil over medium heat until hot, about 1 minute.
3. Add broccoli, season to taste with salt and pepper, and sauté, shaking pan occasionally, 5 to 8 minutes, or just until crisp-tender.
4. Turn broccoli into heatproof bowl and keep warm in 200-degree oven until ready to serve.

Lentils Vinaigrette

½ pound brown lentils (about 1 cup)
Medium-size onion
Medium-size carrot
1 bay leaf
2 sprigs fresh thyme, or ½ teaspoon dried
2 sprigs parsley, plus 2 tablespoons chopped parsley
Salt
3 tablespoons vegetable oil
1½ tablespoons white wine vinegar
1 clove garlic, finely chopped
3 shallots, finely chopped
Freshly ground pepper
Small red bell pepper

1. Place lentils in colander and rinse under cold running water; pick over carefully.
2. Peel and quarter onion. Wash and peel carrot; cut crosswise into 4 pieces.
3. In a double thickness of cheesecloth, tie together bay leaf, thyme, and 2 sprigs parsley for *bouquet garni*.
4. Place lentils in large saucepan with enough cold water to cover. Add onion, carrot, and *bouquet garni*. Season to taste with salt and bring to a simmer, uncovered, over medium-low heat. Continue to simmer gently 45 minutes, checking occasionally to replenish water if necessary.
5. In small bowl, combine oil, vinegar, garlic, shallots, and salt and pepper to taste, and beat with fork until blended.
6. Wash red bell pepper and dry with paper towel. Core, halve, and seed pepper. Cut into ¼-inch dice; set aside.
7. Discard onion, carrot, and *bouquet garni*. Turn lentils into strainer, drain, and transfer to large bowl.
8. Stir vinaigrette to recombine and pour over lentils; toss to combine. Divide lentils among dinner plates and sprinkle with diced bell pepper and chopped parsley.

70

Braised Duck with Onions
Zucchini Flan
Belgian Endive and Orange Salad

A good red wine complements braised duck with onions, slices of zucchini flan, and a Belgian endive and orange salad.

Zucchini are at their peak during the summer months but are available at supermarkets throughout the year. For the zucchini flan, select small squash, about 4 inches long, with glossy, deep green unblemished skin (large zucchini are too coarse and seedy). If you do not plan to use the zucchini immediately, store them in a perforated plastic bag in the refrigerator, where they will keep for several days. For this recipe, the skin is left on for added color.

If you have the time, reserve the excess fat from the cavity of the duck and render it yourself (see page 9).

WHAT TO DRINK

A red wine of sufficient character to balance the richness of the duck is essential here. The best choice would be a Châteauneuf-du-Pape from France's Rhône valley. The famous "black" wine of Cahors, if you can find it, would also be suitable.

SHOPPING LIST AND STAPLES

5 pound whole duck
2 pounds onions
3 medium-size zucchini (about 1 pound total weight)
3 large heads Belgian endive
Small bunch watercress for garnish (optional)
3 small oranges
1 lemon
3 large eggs
¼ pound Gruyère cheese
¼ cup duck fat, see page 9 (optional)
5 tablespoons vegetable oil, approximately, plus ¼ cup (if not using duck fat)
Salt and freshly ground black pepper

UTENSILS

Food processor or blender
2 large heavy-gauge skillets
Flameproof casserole or Dutch oven with cover
8-inch ovenproof ring mold or 1-quart soufflé dish
Medium-size bowl
1 small bowl, plus 1 additional (if using processor)
Salad spinner (optional)
Measuring cups and spoons
Cleaver

Chef's knife
Paring knife
2 wooden spoons
Spatula
Whisk
Metal tongs
Grater (if not using processor)
Juicer

START-TO-FINISH STEPS

1. Follow zucchini flan recipe steps 1 through 5.
2. Follow duck recipe steps 1 through 4.
3. Follow zucchini flan recipe steps 6 and 7.
4. While zucchini flan is baking, follow duck recipe step 5.
5. While duck is braising, follow salad recipe steps 1 through 3.
6. Follow zucchini flan recipe step 8, duck recipe step 6, salad recipe step 4, and serve.

RECIPES

Braised Duck with Onions

5 pound whole duck
¼ cup duck fat or vegetable oil
2 pounds onions
Small bunch watercress for garnish (optional)
Salt
Freshly ground black pepper

1. Remove any excess fat from cavity of duck. Trim off neck skin. Chop off wing tips and reserve with neck and gizzard for another use. With cleaver, quarter duck: Turn duck, skin-side up, on cutting surface and cut through the breastbone. Turn duck over, push back breast halves, and cut backbone in two. Next, place each half skin-side up and, feeling for end of rib cage, cut pieces in half just below ribs. Turn quarters skin-side down and, with sharp knife or cleaver, trim excess skin and any visible fat from each piece. Turn pieces over and prick skin lightly with a fork or skewer to help release fat during cooking.
2. In large heavy-gauge skillet, heat 2 tablespoons duck fat or oil over high heat. Add duck and sauté, turning occasionally, until golden and crisp all over, about 15 minutes.
3. Meanwhile, peel onions and cut crosswise into ¼-inch-thick slices to measure about 4 cups. Wash watercress, if

using, and dry in salad spinner or with paper towels. Reserve 4 sprigs for garnish and refrigerate remainder for another use.

4. In flameproof casserole or Dutch oven large enough to hold the duck in a single layer, heat remaining duck fat or oil over medium heat. Add onions and sauté, stirring occasionally, until softened and light golden, about 10 minutes.

5. Transfer duck to casserole and season to taste with salt and pepper. Cover and braise over medium-low heat 20 to 25 minutes, or until still somewhat rare and juice runs faintly pink.

6. Divide duck among 4 dinner plates, top with onions, and garnish with a sprig of watercress, if desired.

Zucchini Flan

3 medium-size zucchini (about 1 pound total weight)
2 tablespoons vegetable oil, approximately
¼ pound Gruyère cheese
3 large eggs
Salt and freshly ground black pepper

1. Preheat oven to 350 degrees. Line a platter with paper towels.

2. Wash zucchini and dry with paper towels. Trim off ends and discard. Cut crosswise into ½-inch-thick slices. Cut four slices in half for garnish and reserve.

3. In large heavy-gauge skillet, heat 2 tablespoons oil over medium heat. Add zucchini and sauté, stirring occasionally, 8 to 10 minutes, or until softened but not browned.

4. Meanwhile, grate enough cheese in food processor or with grater to measure 1 cup. If using processor, transfer cheese to small bowl. In another small bowl, beat eggs until blended.

5. Transfer sautéed zucchini to paper-towel-lined platter to drain.

6. When drained, place zucchini in food processor fitted with steel blade or in blender and purée. Add eggs, grated cheese, and salt and pepper to taste, and process until blended.

7. Lightly oil an 8-inch ovenproof ring mold or 1-quart soufflé dish. Fill prepared dish three-quarters full with zucchini mixture and bake about 35 minutes, or until knife inserted in center of flan comes out clean.

8. To unmold, run knife around edge of flan while still warm. Place large flat serving plate over mold or dish and invert. Cut flan into 1-inch-thick slices and divide among dinner plates. Garnish with reserved zucchini.

Belgian Endive and Orange Salad

3 large heads Belgian endive
3 small oranges
1 lemon
3 tablespoons vegetable oil
Salt and freshly ground black pepper

1. Remove and discard any bruised outer leaves from endive. Wipe endive with damp paper towels, separate leaves, and place in medium-size bowl.

2. Peel 2 oranges, removing as much white pith as possible. Using very sharp paring knife, cut along membrane on either side of each orange segment. Pull segments apart and place in bowl with endive.

3. Juice remaining orange and half of lemon; reserve remaining half for another use. Combine citrus juices in small bowl, add oil, and salt and pepper to taste, and whisk until blended; set aside.

4. Just before serving, whisk dressing to recombine and pour over endive and oranges. Toss until evenly coated and divide salad among dinner plates.

ADDED TOUCH

This pancake-like fruit pastry is usually made with black cherries, but you may use fresh or canned red cherries.

Cherry Clafouti

1 tablespoon unsalted butter, approximately
¾ cup all-purpose flour
Pinch of salt
2 to 3 tablespoons sugar
4 large eggs
1⅔ cups milk
3 drops vanilla extract
1 pound sweet red cherries, stemmed and pitted, or one 17-ounce can sweet cherries, drained

1. Butter a 10-inch-round gratin dish or pie pan.

2. Preheat oven to 350 degrees.

3. In mixing bowl, sift together flour, salt, and sugar.

4. In medium-size bowl, combine eggs and milk, and whisk until blended. Gradually stir egg mixture into dry ingredients. Stir in vanilla.

5. Turn mixture into prepared baking dish. Distribute cherries evenly over batter and bake in center of oven about 35 minutes, or until clafouti is set in the middle.

6. Cut clafouti into wedges and serve warm or cold.

Jenifer Harvey Lang

MENU 1 (Left)
Sauerkraut-Bean Soup
Viennese-style Turkey Cutlets
Mushroom and Bell Pepper Salad

MENU 2
Hungarian Turkey Terrine
Sautéed Squash with Sour Cream
Baked Stuffed Apples

MENU 3
Sautéed Turkey Cutlets
Lecsó
Rice and Peas

Over the years, Jenifer Harvey Lang has come to prefer honest, uncomplicated food. After marrying restaurateur George Lang and traveling with him in his native Hungary, she discovered that the cuisine of that country suited her taste. All three of her menus typify meals you might eat in eastern European homes. "This is down-to-earth cooking," she says, "that will leave your guests full and immensely satisfied."

Menu 1 starts with a sauerkraut and bean soup, followed by Viennese-style turkey cutlets (*Wienerschnitzel*). *Schnitzel* is a thin slice of boneless meat, usually veal. Here, pounded scallops of turkey are dipped into beaten egg, then into bread crumbs, and are sautéed quickly—just as the classic veal dish is prepared. An easy-to-assemble mushroom and bell pepper salad completes the meal.

A Hungarian terrine, or *fasirt* (pronounced fash-*eert*), made of turkey is the main course of Menu 2, an ideal lunch for company. Sautéed squash complements this lightly seasoned dish.

Menu 3 features turkey cutlets topped with *lecsó*, a Hungarian vegetable sauté resembling *ratatouille*. The cook also serves the *lecsó* on the side.

Bright flowers and a rustic table setting underscore the informality of this Viennese meal. Serve the browned turkey cutlets with slices of tomato and lemon on a large platter, the sauerkraut-bean soup in a lidded tureen, and the mushroom and pepper salad in a wooden bowl.

75

Sauerkraut-Bean Soup
Viennese-style Turkey Cutlets
Mushroom and Bell Pepper Salad

The rich soup contains sauerkraut, lard, and paprika—three common Hungarian ingredients. Sauerkraut, or salted shredded cabbage fermented in its own juice, is best when purchased fresh—you can usually find it at a German delicatessen. A good second choice is sauerkraut sealed in plastic bags, which is available in most supermarkets. Because sauerkraut is pickled, it lasts for a month or longer when stored in a nonmetallic container in the refrigerator. Taste it before using: If it seems too strong, rinse it under cold running water.

Lard, or rendered pork fat, is sold in one-pound blocks at most supermarkets. It refrigerates well for a month and can be frozen for up to a year. The easiest way to measure lard is to cut the block lengthwise into quarters, like sticks of butter, then mark off eight equal sections along each quarter (each section is equal to roughly 1 tablespoon).

For an authentic flavor in the soup, use only imported sweet Hungarian paprika, sold in tins or occasionally in bulk at specialty food stores. The finest paprika is from the town of Szeged and is labeled as such. Spanish paprika (the usual supermarket variety) is not a substitute. Fresh paprika is bright red; brown or faded powder is flavorless. Because paprika loses its delicate flavor quickly, store it in a tightly closed container in the refrigerator.

WHAT TO DRINK

Beer or light ale is the best choice here. A light lager, also called pilsner, would be the most authentic accompaniment for this meal.

SHOPPING LIST AND STAPLES

Eight ¼-inch-thick turkey cutlets (about 2 pounds total weight), pounded to ⅛-inch thickness
¾ pound medium-size or large fresh cultivated mushrooms
Small head Boston lettuce
Large tomato
Small red bell pepper
Small green bell pepper
Small onion
Small bunch thyme or parsley
2 large lemons
16-ounce can red kidney beans
2 large eggs
1 pound fresh sauerkraut, or 16-ounce package
10 tablespoons lard (about ⅓ pound)

½ cup vegetable or peanut oil
1 cup plus 2 tablespoons all-purpose flour
4 slices fresh or stale white bread, approximately
2 teaspoons mild sweet Hungarian paprika
Salt and freshly ground pepper

UTENSILS

Food processor or blender
Large heavy-gauge skillet
Large heavy-gauge saucepan
Wire rack or platter
Ovenproof serving platter
Salad bowl
Large mixing bowl
3 shallow bowls
Colander
Strainer
Measuring cups and spoons
Chef's knife
Paring knife
2 wooden spoons
Juicer
Metal tongs

START-TO-FINISH STEPS

1. Follow salad recipe steps 1 through 4.
2. Follow soup recipe steps 1 through 4.
3. Follow turkey recipe steps 1 through 5.
4. Follow soup recipe step 5.
5. Follow turkey recipe step 6.
6. Follow soup recipe step 6 and serve as first course.
7. Follow salad recipe step 5 and turkey recipe step 7, and serve.

RECIPES

Sauerkraut-Bean Soup

1 pound fresh sauerkraut, or 16-ounce package
Small onion
2 tablespoons lard
2 tablespoons all-purpose flour
2 teaspoons mild sweet Hungarian paprika
1 teaspoon salt
Freshly ground pepper
16-ounce can red kidney beans

1. Place sauerkraut in strainer to drain. Peel and chop enough onion to measure ¼ cup.
2. In large heavy-gauge saucepan, melt lard over medium heat. Stir in flour and cook, stirring continuously, until mixture begins to turn a pale golden brown, about 3 minutes.
3. Add chopped onion and cook, stirring, about 3 minutes, or until onion begins to wilt.
4. Add paprika and cook, stirring, 15 seconds. Add sauerkraut, 4 cups cold water, salt, and pepper to taste, and bring to a boil. Reduce heat to low and simmer, uncovered, 20 minutes, stirring occasionally.
5. Drain kidney beans in colander and rinse under cold running water. Add beans to soup and simmer another 5 minutes.
6. Turn soup into tureen or large serving bowl.

Viennese-style Turkey Cutlets

Large lemon
Large tomato
4 slices fresh or stale white bread, approximately
1 cup all-purpose flour
1 tablespoon salt
1 teaspoon freshly ground pepper
2 large eggs
Eight ¼-inch-thick turkey cutlets (about 2 pounds total weight), pounded to ⅛-inch thickness
8 tablespoons lard
1 sprig fresh parsley for garnish (optional)

1. With paring knife, remove peel and as much white pith as possible from lemon. Cut lemon crosswise into nine ¼-inch-thick slices; set aside. Wash tomato, dry, core, and cut crosswise into eight ¼-inch-thick slices; set aside.
2. Trim crusts from bread. In food processor fitted with steel blade, or in blender, process enough bread to measure about 1 cup crumbs.
3. Combine flour, salt, and pepper in shallow bowl and stir with fork to blend. Crack eggs into another shallow bowl and beat with fork until blended. Turn bread crumbs into third shallow bowl.
4. Preheat oven to 200 degrees.
5. One at a time, dip cutlets into flour, shaking off excess, then into beaten eggs, and then into bread crumbs, coating thoroughly. As coated, place cutlets on wire rack or platter.
6. In large heavy-gauge skillet, melt 4 tablespoons lard

over medium-high heat until quite hot. Add only as many cutlets to skillet as will fit in a single layer and sauté until golden brown, about 30 seconds per side. Reduce heat to medium if lard begins to smoke. When cutlets are cooked, transfer to ovenproof serving platter and keep warm in oven. Add remaining lard and repeat for remaining cutlets.
7. Top each cutlet with 1 slice of tomato and 1 slice of lemon. Garnish platter with remaining slice of lemon and a sprig of parsley, if desired, and serve.

Mushroom and Bell Pepper Salad

¾ pound medium-size or large fresh cultivated mushrooms
Small head Boston lettuce
Small bunch thyme or parsley
Small red bell pepper
Small green bell pepper
Large lemon
1 teaspoon salt
Freshly ground pepper
½ cup vegetable or peanut oil

1. Fill large bowl with cold water and add mushrooms. Bounce mushrooms up and down with your fingers for about 15 seconds to dislodge dirt. With paper towel, gently wipe any mushroom caps that still appear dirty. Remove mushrooms from water, pat dry with paper towels, and cut into halves or quarters. Rinse and dry bowl.
2. Wash lettuce and thyme or parsley, and dry with paper towels. If using thyme, strip enough leaves to measure 1 tablespoon; if using parsley, chop enough to measure 2 tablespoons. Wash and dry bell peppers. Halve, core, and seed peppers; cut lengthwise into 1-inch-long julienne. Squeeze enough lemon juice to measure about ¼ cup. Line salad bowl with lettuce leaves, cover, and refrigerate until ready to serve.
3. In blender or food processor, combine thyme leaves or chopped parsley, 2 tablespoons lemon juice, salt, pepper to taste, and oil, and blend about 15 seconds, or until dressing is smooth and thick. Taste and add more lemon juice if desired.
4. In large mixing bowl, combine mushrooms and peppers. Add dressing and toss to combine. Set aside at room temperature, and stir occasionally.
5. When ready to serve, transfer mushrooms and peppers to lettuce-lined salad bowl.

Hungarian Turkey Terrine
Sautéed Squash with Sour Cream
Baked Stuffed Apples

Slices of turkey terrine and a helping of squash are the entrée for this Hungarian meal, with baked stuffed apples as dessert.

A terrine is an earthenware dish or mold in which a seasoned blend of chopped meat, fish, or vegetables cooks—and it lends its name to the resultant pâté-like loaf. In this Hungarian adaptation of a classic terrine, the turkey mixture cooks freestanding on a greased baking sheet. If you wish to create an elegant mosaic pattern when the cooked terrine is sliced, put half the ground turkey mixture on the baking sheet, place a row of hard-cooked eggs or sections of kielbasa sausage lengthwise down the center, and cover with the remaining turkey. Bake as indicated in the recipe. This terrine can be served hot, cold, or at room temperature.

WHAT TO DRINK

A crisp, flavorful white wine with a touch of spiciness makes an excellent partner for these dishes. Try an Alsatian or California Gewürztraminer, or, if you want a red wine, perhaps a lightly chilled Beaujolais.

SHOPPING LIST AND STAPLES

2 pounds ground turkey
4 slices bacon (about ¼ pound)
2 medium-size yellow crookneck or zucchini squash (about 1 pound total weight)
Medium-size onion plus 1 small onion
Small bunch parsley
Small bunch dill
4 firm apples
1 lemon for garnish (optional)
1 lime for garnish (optional)
2 large eggs
½ cup milk
½ pint sour cream
1½ tablespoons unsalted butter
1 tablespoon white vinegar
12-ounce jar currant jelly
2 slices fresh or stale white bread
1 tablespoon all-purpose flour
3-ounce can walnut or pecan pieces, or 4-ounce can slivered almonds
1 teaspoon mild sweet Hungarian paprika
Salt and freshly ground pepper

UTENSILS

Food processor or blender
Large heavy-gauge skillet
11 x 17-inch baking sheet with sides
8 x 8-inch baking pan
Large mixing bowl
Shallow bowl
Small mixing bowl
Measuring cups and spoons
Chef's knife
Wooden spoon
2 large metal spatulas
Apple corer
Grater (if not using processor)
Nut grinder (if not using processor)

START-TO-FINISH STEPS

1. Follow turkey recipe step 1.
2. Follow apples recipe steps 1 through 4.
3. While apples are baking, follow turkey recipe steps 2 through 6.
4. Follow squash recipe step 1 and apples recipe steps 5 and 6.
5. Follow turkey recipe step 7 and squash recipe steps 2 through 6.
6. Follow turkey recipe step 8 and serve with squash.
7. Follow apples recipe step 7 and serve as dessert.

RECIPES

Hungarian Turkey Terrine

2 slices fresh or stale white bread
½ cup milk
Medium-size onion
Small bunch parsley
4 slices bacon (about ¼ pound)
2 large eggs
1 teaspoon mild sweet Hungarian paprika
1 teaspoon salt
Freshly ground pepper to taste
2 pounds ground turkey

1. Preheat oven to 375 degrees.
2. Place bread in a shallow bowl; pour milk over bread and set aside to soak 5 to 10 minutes.
3. Meanwhile, peel onion and cut into 8 pieces. Wash parsley and dry with paper towels; chop enough to measure ⅓ cup.
4. Place soaked bread (discarding any unabsorbed milk), onion, parsley, and all remaining ingredients except ground turkey in food processor fitted with steel blade, or in blender, and process just until combined.
5. In large mixing bowl, combine ground turkey and ingredients from food processor and mix with your hands until well blended.
6. Generously oil large rectangular baking sheet with sides. Turn terrine mixture out onto prepared sheet and shape into rounded 12 x 4-inch loaf that is about 3 inches high. Smooth top and bake 20 minutes.
7. Increase oven temperature to 450 degrees and bake loaf another 10 minutes, or until juices are clear (not pink).
8. Using 2 large metal spatulas, transfer terrine to cutting surface. Cut into ¾-inch-thick slices and divide among dinner plates.

Sautéed Squash with Sour Cream

2 medium-size yellow crookneck or zucchini squash (about 1 pound total weight)
Small onion
Small bunch dill

1½ tablespoons unsalted butter
1 tablespoon all-purpose flour
1 tablespoon white vinegar
1 teaspoon salt
¼ cup sour cream

1. In food processor fitted with grating disk, or on coarse side of grater, grate squash. Peel and mince onion. Wash dill and dry with paper towel; chop enough to measure 1 tablespoon.
2. In large heavy-gauge skillet, melt butter over medium heat. Stir in flour to make a smooth paste and cook, stirring, until mixture begins to turn light brown, about 2 minutes.
3. Add onion and sauté, stirring, 3 minutes, or until onion begins to wilt.
4. Add grated squash, vinegar, and salt, and sauté, stirring, another 2 minutes.
5. Add sour cream and cook, stirring, 30 seconds.
6. Divide squash among 4 dinner plates and sprinkle with chopped dill.

Baked Stuffed Apples

4 firm apples
3-ounce can walnut or pecan pieces, or 4-ounce can
    slivered almonds
¼ cup currant jelly
1 lemon for garnish (optional)
1 lime for garnish (optional)

1. Wash apples and dry with paper towels. With apple corer, core apples without cutting through bottoms; do not peel. Using food processor or nut grinder, grind enough nuts to measure ½ cup.
2. Oil an 8 x 8-inch baking pan. Fit apples snugly into the pan.
3. Combine ground nuts and currant jelly in small bowl. Spoon one-quarter of mixture into each apple.
4. Bake apples in 375-degree oven 30 minutes.
5. Wash lemon and lime, if using, and dry with paper towels. Slice four ¼-inch-thick slices from lemon and reserve remaining lemon for another use. Cut four ⅛-inch-thick rounds from lime; stack rounds and cut a notch halfway through diameter, so that lime will stand up when twisted.
6. Remove apples from oven, cover loosely with foil, and set aside until ready to serve.

7. When ready to serve, transfer apples to dessert plates and garnish each serving with a lemon slice and a lime twist, if desired.

ADDED TOUCH

Use fresh or frozen chicken or turkey carcasses to make the stock for this flavorful soup. For maximum flavor, select deep red and firm fresh beets of small or medium size; large beets tend to be coarse.

Beet Soup

5 medium-size fresh beets (about 1½ pounds total weight)
1 lemon
1½ tablespoons lard
2 tablespoons all-purpose flour
4 cups chicken or turkey stock, preferably homemade
    (see page 11), or canned
1 teaspoon caraway seeds
½ teaspoon salt
Freshly ground pepper
2 or 3 sweet Italian sausages or frankfurters (about 6
    ounces total weight)
½ cup sour cream
2 tablespoons milk

1. Trim off tops of beets and reserve for another use. Wash and peel beets and cut enough into ½-inch dice to measure about 4 cups. Cut lemon in half, squeeze juice from one half, and set aside. Reserve remaining half for another use.
2. In large heavy-gauge saucepan, melt lard over medium heat. Stir in flour and cook, stirring, until mixture begins to turn pale golden brown, about 3 minutes.
3. Add chicken or turkey stock, beets, lemon juice, caraway seeds, salt, and pepper to taste, and bring to a boil over high heat. Reduce heat to low and simmer, uncovered, 15 minutes, or until beets are cooked.
4. Meanwhile, cut sausages into ¼-inch-thick slices. In medium-size skillet, sauté sausages over medium-high heat, stirring, 8 to 10 minutes, or until browned on both sides; transfer to paper towels to drain.
5. When beets are cooked, add browned sausages to soup and stir just to combine.
6. Combine sour cream and milk in small bowl and stir until blended. Divide soup among 4 individual bowls and top each serving with a generous spoonful of sour cream mixture.

Sautéed Turkey Cutlets
Lecsó
Rice and Peas

Spoon some lecsó *over the cutlets, then offer the rest in a separate bowl. Rice and peas provide additional texture.*

In Hungary, *lecsó* is served hot or cold, spicy or mild. It can also be a topping for cutlets, as in this menu; an accompaniment to omelets; or a meal in itself with the addition of sausage, meat, or eggs. If you are fond of piquant foods, you can add extra fire by chopping up and stirring in a hot Mexican jalapeño or serrano chili pepper. Or, you can add 1 tablespoon of chopped dried chili pepper, ½ teaspoon of Cayenne pepper, or some hot pepper sauce, along with the paprika in step 5 of the recipe. *Lecsó* should be stewed slowly so that all the flavors meld.

For extra texture, the cook recommends garnishing the *lecsó* (and the rice) with turkey cracklings (for information on cracklings, see page 62). If you make the cracklings ahead and store them in the refrigerator, you can re-crisp them by moistening with a few drops of water and cooking them in a covered skillet.

WHAT TO DRINK

Red wine is appropriate with the cutlets, and the cook suggests the Hungarian favorite Egri Bikavér. If it is not available, try a California Zinfandel.

SHOPPING LIST AND STAPLES

Eight ½-inch-thick turkey cutlets (about 2 pounds total weight)
4 green, red, or yellow bell peppers, or 1½ pounds long Italian frying peppers

81

1 pound very ripe plum tomatoes, or 16-ounce can Italian
    plum tomatoes
3 large onions (about 2¼ pounds total weight)
Small hot chili pepper (optional)
2 large lemons
⅓ cup beef stock (optional)
2 cups chicken stock, preferably homemade (see
    page 11), or canned, plus ⅓ cup additional (if not using
    beef stock)
4 tablespoons lard
10-ounce package frozen peas
¾ cup vegetable oil, approximately
1 cup long-grain white rice
1 teaspoon sugar
1 tablespoon mild sweet Hungarian paprika
1 bay leaf
Salt
Freshly ground pepper

UTENSILS

Food processor or blender
2 large heavy-gauge skillets, 1 ovenproof and 1 with cover
Large heavy-gauge saucepan with tight-fitting cover
Ovenproof serving platter
Ovenproof serving bowl
Strainer
Measuring cups and spoons
Chef's knife
2 wooden spoons
Metal tongs
Juicer

START-TO-FINISH STEPS

1. Peel and slice enough onions to measure 3 cups for lecsó
recipe. Mince enough onion to measure 1 cup for rice and
peas recipe.
2. Follow lecsó recipe steps 1 through 4.
3. While vegetables are cooking, follow rice and peas
recipe steps 1 through 3.
4. Follow turkey recipe steps 1 and 2, and lecsó recipe
step 5.
5. Follow rice and peas recipe steps 4 and 5.
6. Follow lecsó recipe step 6.
7. Follow turkey recipe steps 3 through 6, rice and peas
recipe step 6, and serve with lecsó.

82

RECIPES

Sautéed Turkey Cutlets

2 large lemons
½ cup vegetable oil, approximately
Eight ½-inch-thick turkey cutlets (about 2 pounds
    total weight)
Salt
Freshly ground pepper
⅓ cup chicken or beef stock
Lecsó (see following recipe)

1. Preheat oven to 200 degrees.
2. Squeeze enough lemon juice to measure ⅓ cup.
3. Heat enough oil to cover bottom of large ovenproof
heavy-gauge skillet over medium-high heat. Add only as
many cutlets to pan as will fit in a single layer, and sauté
until light brown, 2 to 3 minutes per side. Reduce heat to
medium if oil begins to smoke.
4. When cutlets are cooked, transfer to ovenproof serving
platter and sprinkle with salt and pepper. Keep warm in
oven. Repeat for remaining cutlets. Pour off all but 2
tablespoons oil from skillet.
5. Add stock and lemon juice to skillet and bring to a boil
over high heat. Cook, scraping up browned bits that cling
to bottom of pan, until liquid is reduced by half, about
5 minutes.
6. Spoon sauce over cutlets and top with some of the lecsó.

Lecsó

4 tablespoons lard
3 cups sliced onions
4 green, red, or yellow bell peppers, or 1½ pounds long
    Italian frying peppers
Small hot chili pepper (optional)
1 pound very ripe plum tomatoes, or 16-ounce can Italian
    plum tomatoes
1 tablespoon mild sweet Hungarian paprika
2 teaspoons salt
1 teaspoon sugar

1. In large heavy-gauge skillet, melt lard over medium
heat. Add onions and sauté, stirring occasionally, 5 to 8
minutes, or until very soft and translucent.
2. Meanwhile, wash peppers and dry with paper towels.
Halve, core, and seed bell peppers; cut into ¼-inch-wide
strips. If using chili pepper, wearing rubber gloves, halve

lengthwise; remove seeds with tip of knife for less fiery flavor, if desired. Dice chili.

3. When onions are cooked, stir in bell peppers, and chili pepper if using. Reduce heat to low, cover, and cook, stirring occasionally, 15 to 20 minutes, or until peppers are very soft.

4. Meanwhile, if using fresh tomatoes, wash, and dry with paper towels. Remove stem ends from tomatoes and discard. Quarter fresh tomatoes and purée in food processor fitted with steel blade, or in blender. If using canned tomatoes, do not drain; purée in food processor or blender.

5. Add paprika, salt, and sugar to peppers and onions and cook, stirring, about 1 minute. Stir in puréed tomatoes, increase heat to medium, and simmer, stirring occasionally, about 8 minutes, or until mixture is medium-thick.

6. Turn lecsó into ovenproof serving bowl and keep warm in 200-degree oven until ready to serve.

Rice and Peas

¼ cup vegetable oil
1 cup minced onion
1 cup long-grain white rice
2 cups chicken stock
1 bay leaf
¾ teaspoon salt
Freshly ground pepper
1 cup frozen peas

1. In large heavy-gauge saucepan, heat oil over medium heat. Add onion and sauté, stirring, 3 to 5 minutes, or until soft and translucent.

2. Add rice and stir until evenly coated with oil.

3. Stir in stock, bay leaf, salt, and pepper to taste. Increase heat to high and bring to a boil. Reduce heat to very low, cover tightly, and simmer 15 minutes.

4. Place peas in strainer and rinse under cold water to separate. Remove bay leaf from rice and discard. Stir in peas, cover, and cook another 3 minutes.

5. Turn off heat and keep rice and peas warm, covered, until ready to serve.

6. Fluff rice and peas with fork and turn into serving bowl.

ADDED TOUCH

This steamed pudding cooks for several hours in a coffee can. After steaming, you can serve it immediately, let it cool to room temperature, or chill it. The colder the pudding, the denser and more chocolaty it becomes. Be sure to top it with whipped cream.

Steamed Chocolate-Almond Pudding

3 eggs, at room temperature
1 ounce (1 square) semisweet chocolate
5 tablespoons unsalted butter
⅓ cup plus 1 tablespoon sugar
2 tablespoons bread crumbs, preferably homemade
1 tablespoon rum
5 tablespoons ground unblanched almonds
Vegetable cooking spray or butter for greasing coffee can
1 cup heavy cream
1 teaspoon vanilla extract

1. Separate eggs into 2 small bowls. With electric mixer at high speed, beat whites until stiff.

2. Place chocolate in top of double boiler set over, not in, barely simmering water. Cover double boiler and remove from heat. Bring a kettle of water to a boil.

3. Combine butter and ⅓ cup sugar in large bowl and beat with electric mixer at medium speed about 3 minutes, or until light and fluffy.

4. While beating, gradually add egg yolks to mixture and continue to beat until totally incorporated.

5. In small bowl, combine bread crumbs and rum. Add crumb mixture and ground almonds to pudding and beat 30 seconds.

6. Stir chocolate to make sure it has melted completely. Add to pudding and beat until incorporated.

7. Using rubber spatula, fold in egg whites until totally incorporated and no streaks of white remain.

8. Coat inside of clean 1-pound coffee can with vegetable cooking spray or small amount of butter. Pour in pudding batter and tightly cover coffee can with a quadruple layer of foil tied around the top.

9. Place coffee can in saucepan or Dutch oven at least 5½ inches deep. Add enough boiling water to reach halfway up the sides of can. Place pan over medium-low heat, cover, and steam pudding 1 hour and 20 minutes.

10. To test for doneness, remove foil and press top of pudding with your finger. If the top springs back, pudding is cooked. Invert can to unmold pudding.

11. When ready to serve, cut pudding crosswise into four equal slices and place each slice on a dessert plate.

12. Beat heavy cream with vanilla and remaining sugar until very thick but not stiff. Top each slice of pudding with a generous spoonful of whipped cream and serve.

Bruce Aidells

MENU 1 (Right)
Mexican Turkey Salad
Herbed Cheese Spread
Wild Rice and Walnut Salad

MENU 2
Turkey Pontalba
Sautéed Zucchini Noodles

MENU 3
Creole-style Duck
Dirty Rice
Bittersweet Tossed Salad

ruce Aidells is an enthusiastic cook who describes his food as substantial and lavishly seasoned. He enjoys cooking the spirited dishes of Mexico, and in the past few years, he has also been experimenting with Louisiana's Creole and Cajun cuisines, which are inspired by French, English, native American, Spanish, and African cooking.

His Menu 1 features a Mexican-style turkey salad, a wild rice salad, and a Creole-inspired herbed cheese spread, all excellent for a picnic lunch or light supper because they can be prepared in advance.

Menus 2 and 3 also include hearty dishes from Louisiana. The entrée for Menu 2 is a turkey dish named for a famous New Orleans Creole family, also commemorated by the historic Pontalba buildings in the French Quarter. This dish contrasts mild turkey cutlets with a spicy potato and sausage mixture and a peppery Béarnaise sauce. With the turkey, the cook serves a zucchini sauté redolent with garlic.

In Menu 3, pieces of duck are covered with a thick Creole sauce that includes bell peppers, onions, tomatoes, and Cayenne pepper. Dirty rice, a Cajun favorite that got its name from the ground giblets that fleck it, goes with the zesty main course.

For an attractive buffet, mound the lightly dressed turkey salad in the center of an earthenware bowl and surround it with cherry tomatoes. Serve the wild rice salad in a separate bowl and the herbed cheese spread with a basket of unsalted crackers.

Turkey Pontalba
Sautéed Zucchini Noodles

Take your guests down South with a Creole entrée of sautéed turkey cutlets with Béarnaise sauce served over a portion of andouille *sausage and cubed potatoes. Shredded zucchini flavored with sliced* pancetta *and garlic is the accompaniment.*

The Louisiana *andouille* sausage used in the entrée gives the potato mixture a distinctive smoky flavor. Unlike the French *andouille,* this American version is made with pork meat rather than intestines. It is highly seasoned with garlic and Cayenne pepper before being smoked. You can substitute Polish *kielbasa* or Portuguese *linguiça* sausages instead, but these lack the intense flavor of *andouille.* (See page 103 for mail-order sources for *andouille* sausage.)

The zucchini noodles are not noodles at all but finely julienned zucchini; to slice them, the cook suggests using a mandoline—a simple set of blades fixed to a frame. Move the zucchini rhythmically across the blades, pushing with the heel of your hand. If you do not have a mandoline, use a food processor fitted with a shredding disk, or a grater. If using a processor, be sure to cut the zucchini to fit the feed tube when inserted horizontally; this ensures long, noodle-like shreds. Salting the zucchini draws out water and gives the cooked vegetables a chewy texture—like pasta cooked *al dente.*

WHAT TO DRINK

This New Orleans-style menu would be well matched with a fruity white Gewürztraminer or Chenin Blanc, or a red Italian Dolcetto or California Gamay Beaujolais.

SHOPPING LIST AND STAPLES

Four ¼-inch-thick turkey cutlets (about 1 pound total weight)
½ pound Louisiana andouille sausage or other smoked sausage, such as kielbasa or linguiça
¼ pound pancetta or bacon
3 medium-size zucchini (1½ to 2 pounds total weight)
1 pound red or white boiling potatoes
Medium-size yellow onion
Small bunch scallions
¼ pound mushrooms
2 large shallots
3 cloves garlic
Small bunch parsley
Small bunch chervil (optional)
1 lemon
3 large eggs
2 sticks plus 2 tablespoons unsalted butter
3 tablespoons olive oil

2 cups peanut oil or other oil for frying
2-ounce bottle hot pepper sauce
1 cup all-purpose flour
1 teaspoon dried tarragon
¾ teaspoon Cayenne pepper, approximately
½ teaspoon dried thyme
Salt
2 tablespoons kosher salt
Freshly ground black pepper
¾ cup dry white wine

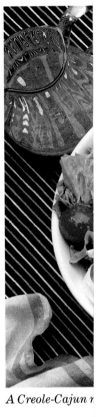

Because the c
to the sauc
making the dish
Creole recipe wi
thighs. Fresh p
early fall—are p

You can serve
either before or
include tart esc
and mild leaf let
to mild ratio the
mustard, a coa
cludes horserac
food shops.

For the dirty
cause its taste a
method for pre
directly to the c
for a minute or t
to 20 minutes. I
1¼ cups since th

UTENSILS

Mandoline, food processor, or grater
Large heavy-gauge skillet
Medium-size heavy-gauge skillet
Large sauté pan
Double boiler with nonaluminum top
2 small saucepans, 1 nonaluminum
13 x 9-inch baking dish
9-inch pie pan
Small bowl
Colander
Strainer
Measuring cups and spoons
Chef's knife
Paring knife
2 wooden spoons
Metal spatula
Whisk
Metal tongs
Juicer (optional)

START-TO-FINISH STEPS

1. Squeeze enough lemon juice to measure 1 tablespoon for Béarnaise sauce recipe and 2 teaspoons for zucchini recipe. Peel and mince enough garlic to measure 1 tablespoon for turkey recipe and 2 teaspoons for zucchini recipe. Peel and finely chop shallots for sauce recipe. Wash, dry, and chop enough parsley to measure ¼ cup for turkey recipe, and 1 tablespoon for Béarnaise sauce recipe if not using chervil.
2. Follow zucchini recipe steps 1 and 2.
3. Follow turkey recipe steps 1 through 11.
4. Follow Béarnaise sauce recipe steps 1 through 7.
5. Follow zucchini recipe steps 3 through 8.
6. Follow turkey recipe step 12 and serve with zucchini noodles.

RECIPES

Turkey Pontalba

½ pound Louisiana andouille sausage or other smoked
    sausage, such as kielbasa or linguiça
Medium-size yellow onion
1 pound red or white boiling potatoes

¼ pound mushrooms
2 tablespoons unsalted butter
1 tablespoon olive oil
4 scallions
Salt
Freshly ground black pepper
¾ teaspoon Cayenne pepper, approximately
1 cup all-purpose flour
Four ¼-inch-thick turkey cutlets (about 1 pound total
    weight)
2 cups peanut oil or other oil for frying
1 tablespoon minced garlic
½ cup dry white wine
½ teaspoon dried thyme
¼ cup chopped parsley
Béarnaise Sauce (see following recipe)

1. Cut sausage into ¼-inch dice. Peel and finely chop enough onion to measure 1 cup. Wash potatoes under cold running water and dry; cut into ½-inch dice to measure about 4 cups. Wipe mushrooms clean with damp paper towels and slice thinly to measure about 1 cup.
2. In medium-size heavy-gauge skillet, combine butter and olive oil over medium heat. Add sausage and sauté, stirring occasionally, 5 minutes.
3. Meanwhile, wash scallions and dry with paper towels. Trim off ends and thinly slice enough scallions to measure ½ cup; set aside.
4. Add onion and potatoes to skillet with sausage and sauté over medium-high heat, stirring occasionally, about 15 minutes, or until vegetables are lightly browned.
5. Preheat oven to 200 degrees. Line a platter with paper towels.
6. While vegetables are cooking, combine ¼ teaspoon salt, ½ teaspoon pepper, and a pinch of Cayenne in small bowl. Combine flour, ½ teaspoon salt, ½ teaspoon pepper, and a pinch of Cayenne in pie pan.
7. Rinse cutlets under cold running water and dry with paper towels.
8. In large heavy-gauge skillet, heat peanut oil over medium heat.
9. While oil is heating, season cutlets on both sides with mixture from small bowl; then dredge each cutlet in seasoned flour and gently shake off excess. Add two cutlets to pan and fry 2 to 3 minutes per side, or until golden. As they are done, transfer cutlets to paper-towel-lined platter. Repeat for remaining two cutlets.
10. Add mushrooms, garlic, white wine, thyme, and ½ teaspoon Cayenne to sausage-vegetable mixture, and stir to combine. Season mixture to taste with salt and black pepper, and sauté over high heat, stirring, 3 to 4 minutes.
11. Stir in scallions and sprinkle with parsley. Turn mixture into baking dish and place cutlets on top. Cover loosely with foil and keep warm in oven until ready to serve.
12. Divide potato-sausage mixture with cutlets among 4 dinner plates. Top each cutlet with a generous spoonful of Béarnaise sauce.

Béarnaise S

2 sticks unsalte
Small bunch ch
2 large shallots
1 tablespoon ch
¼ cup dry white
1 tablespoon ler
1 teaspoon drie
¼ teaspoon salt
¼ teaspoon fres
3 large eggs
Hot pepper sau

1. Melt butter i
2. If using, wa
Finely chop en
serving remain
3. In small noi
shallots, chervi
ragon, salt, and
high heat. Cont
is reduced to 2
4. Bring 1 quar
double boiler ov
5. Separate egg
double boiler ai
hot pepper sauc
barely simmerii
begin to thicker
6. Pour reduced
until blended.
7. Whisking coi
steady stream
slightly thicken
set aside until i

Sautéed Zuc

3 medium-size z
2 tablespoons ko
¼ pound pancet
2 tablespoons ol
2 teaspoons min
2 teaspoons lem
Freshly ground

1. Wash zucchin
and discard. Us
shredding disk,
shreds possible.
2. Transfer zuc
toss until evenl
minutes.
3. Cut pancetta
4. In large saute
pancetta and fr
5. Meanwhile, i
Squeeze out ex
6. Add garlic to

---

2 small green bell peppers
Small bunch celery
2 medium-size onions (about 1 pound total weight)
Small bunch scallions
1 leek
12 small cloves garlic
2½ cups duck or chicken stock, preferably homemade
  (see page 11), or two 13¾-ounce cans
6 tablespoons unsalted butter
1¼ cups olive oil
¼ cup sherry vinegar
1 tablespoon Creole or other coarse-grained mustard
½ teaspoon Worcestershire sauce
2-ounce bottle hot pepper sauce
1 cup converted long-grain rice
1¼ teaspoons dried thyme
¾ teaspoon dried sage
½ teaspoon paprika
½ teaspoon dried sweet basil
¼ teaspoon dried oregano
2 bay leaves
1 teaspoon Cayenne pepper, approximately
Salt
Freshly ground black pepper

UTENSILS

Food processor, blender, or meat grinder
Large heavy-gauge skillet
Large sauté pan
Medium-size heavy-gauge saucepan with cover
13 x 9-inch roasting pan with rack
Large ovenproof serving dish
3 small bowls
Salad spinner (optional)
Measuring cups and spoons
Chef's knife
Cleaver (optional)
Paring knife
2 wooden spoons
Metal spatula
Rubber spatula
Small whisk
Metal tongs
Metal skewer (optional)

START-TO-FINISH STEPS

1. Wash bell peppers and celery, and dry with paper towels. Core, halve, and seed peppers; dice finely. Trim off and discard ends of celery stalks; dice finely. Peel onions; cut 1 onion crosswise into thin slices for sauce recipe and finely dice remaining onion for rice recipe. Peel and mince garlic for rice, salad, and sauce recipes. Wash and dry fresh plum tomatoes, if using, for duck recipe and cherry tomatoes for salad recipe. Remove stems from cherry tomatoes, if necessary, and cut tomatoes in half. Coarsely chop plum tomatoes to measure 2½ cups.

---

2. Follow duck recipe steps 1 through 8.
3. While onion is cooking, follow rice recipe steps 1 through 3.
4. Follow duck recipe steps 9 through 12.
5. While duck is cooking, follow rice recipe steps 4 and 5, and salad recipe steps 1 and 2.
6. Follow rice recipe steps 6 through 12, and duck recipe step 13.
7. Follow rice recipe steps 13 and 14.
8. Follow salad recipe step 3, rice recipe step 15, and serve with duck.

RECIPES

Creole-style Duck

3½- to 5-pound duck
½ teaspoon paprika
¼ teaspoon dried sage
¼ teaspoon dried thyme
¼ teaspoon dried oregano
Pinch of Cayenne pepper
½ teaspoon salt
½ teaspoon freshly ground black pepper

Creole Sauce:

¼ pound smoked ham or sausage, such as Louisiana
  andouille, kielbasa, or linguiça
2 tablespoons unsalted butter
Small bunch scallions
Medium-size onion, peeled and thinly sliced
Small green bell pepper, finely diced
2 stalks celery, finely diced
4 small cloves garlic, minced (about 1 tablespoon)
10 plum tomatoes, coarsely chopped (about 2½ cups),
  or 16-ounce can plum tomatoes in purée
1 cup duck or chicken stock
½ teaspoon dried thyme
½ teaspoon dried sweet basil
¼ teaspoon dried sage
½ teaspoon Cayenne pepper
2 bay leaves
Salt
Freshly ground black pepper
½ teaspoon Worcestershire sauce
Hot pepper sauce

1. Preheat oven to 450 degrees. Place rack in roasting pan.
2. Rinse duck under cold running water and dry with paper towels. Remove any excess fat from cavity of duck. Trim off neck skin. Chop off wing tips and reserve with neck skin for stock. With heavy cleaver or chef's knife, quarter duck: Place duck breast-side up and cut through keel bone. Push back breast halves to expose backbone and cut in two. Next, place each half, skin-side up, on cutting surface and, feeling for end of rib cage, cut each piece crosswise in half. Turn quarters skin-side down and trim skin and any visible fat from edges of each piece.
3. In small bowl, combine herbs and spices, and stir with

fork until blended. Rub both sides of duck quarters with herb-spice mixture.

4. Prick skin with metal skewer or fork in several places to help release fat during cooking. Place duck pieces on rack and roast 30 to 35 minutes.

5. While duck is roasting, to prepare Creole sauce, finely dice ham or sausage.

6. Heat butter in large heavy-gauge skillet over medium heat. Add ham or sausage and fry 3 to 5 minutes.

7. Meanwhile, wash scallions, dry with paper towels, and trim off ends and discard. Slice scallions thinly to measure about 1 cup; set aside.

8. Add onion to skillet and sauté over high heat, stirring occasionally, 5 minutes, or until lightly browned.

9. Stir in green pepper and celery, and sauté 2 minutes, or until limp.

10. Stir in garlic and scallions, and sauté 1 minute.

11. Reduce heat to medium and stir in tomatoes, stock, thyme, basil, sage, Cayenne, bay leaves, and salt and pepper to taste.

12. Remove duck from oven. Reduce oven temperature to 200 degrees. Add duck to skillet with Creole sauce and simmer vigorously, uncovered, 15 to 20 minutes.

13. To test duck for doneness, pierce with tip of knife; if juices run clear, turn duck into large ovenproof serving dish. Remove bay leaves from sauce; stir in Worcestershire and hot pepper sauce to taste. Adjust seasoning and pour sauce over duck. Cover dish loosely with foil, and keep warm in oven until ready to serve.

Dirty Rice

1½ cups duck or chicken stock
Small eggplant (about 1 pound)
1 cup converted long-grain rice
¼ cup olive oil
Gizzard, heart, and liver from duck
4 tablespoons unsalted butter
¼ pound mushrooms
Medium-size onion, peeled and finely diced
1 leek
Small green bell pepper, finely diced
1 stalk celery, finely diced
4 small cloves garlic, minced (about 1 tablespoon)
½ teaspoon Cayenne pepper
½ teaspoon dried thyme
¼ teaspoon dried sage
Salt
Freshly ground black pepper

1. Bring stock to a boil in medium-size heavy-gauge saucepan over high heat.

2. While stock is heating, wash eggplant and dry with paper towels. Trim off ends and discard; cut into ½-inch dice to measure about 4 cups.

3. Add rice to boiling stock, cover pan, and reduce heat to medium-low. Simmer gently 20 minutes, or until stock is absorbed and rice is tender.

4. In large sauté pan, heat olive oil over medium heat. Add eggplant and sauté, stirring occasionally, about 10 minutes, or until soft.

5. While eggplant is cooking, rinse gizzard, heart, and liver under cold running water and dry. In food processor fitted with steel blade, in blender, or with meat grinder, grind gizzard and heart; turn into small bowl. Grind liver; set aside separately.

6. Turn cooked eggplant into another small bowl; rinse and dry sauté pan.

7. Add butter to pan and heat over medium heat. Add gizzard and heart, and sauté 3 to 5 minutes, or until they lose their raw look.

8. Meanwhile, wipe mushrooms clean with damp paper towels and slice thinly.

9. Add onion to sauté pan and cook, stirring occasionally, 5 minutes, or until soft.

10. Meanwhile, trim off ends of leek, leaving 2 to 3 inches of green top. Cut leek lengthwise to within 1 inch of root end. Gently spread leaves and rinse thoroughly under cold running water to remove all sand and grit. Dry leek with paper towels and cut crosswise into ¼-inch-thick pieces.

11. Add green pepper, celery, and leek to onion mixture, stir, and sauté 2 to 3 minutes.

12. Stir in mushrooms, garlic, Cayenne, thyme, sage, and salt and pepper to taste, and sauté until leek is soft, about 3 to 4 minutes.

13. Add liver and sauté, stirring occasionally, another 5 minutes.

14. Stir in cooked rice and eggplant, and cook gently over low heat 5 to 10 minutes, or until heated through.

15. Turn rice into serving dish.

Bittersweet Tossed Salad

¼ head chicory or other bitter green
¼ head Bibb lettuce or other mild green
¼ head red leaf lettuce or other mild green
¼ cup sherry vinegar
1 tablespoon Creole or other coarse-grained
  mustard
4 small cloves garlic, minced (about 1 tablespoon)
½ teaspoon salt
Freshly ground black pepper
1 cup olive oil
12 cherry tomatoes, halved

1. Wash greens and dry in salad spinner or with paper towels. Remove and discard any bruised or discolored leaves. Wrap greens in paper towels and refrigerate until ready to serve.

2. In small bowl, combine vinegar, mustard, garlic, salt, and pepper to taste, and whisk until blended. Whisking continuously, add oil in a slow, steady stream and whisk until dressing is well blended and creamy.

3. Combine greens and tomatoes in salad bowl. Stir dressing to recombine. Add half the dressing to salad and toss until evenly coated. Serve salad with extra dressing in a small bowl or pitcher on the side.

Jeanne Marie Voltz

F ine food has always been an important part of Jeanne Marie Voltz's life. Through her parents, she was continually exposed not only to southern cooking but also to many other American regional and European cuisines. Her menus reflect her southern background, with a dash of California and Europe thrown in. All are excellent company fare.

Menu 1, a year-round party meal, begins with a long-time southern favorite, peanut soup—a variation on a recipe created by George Washington Carver, who promoted peanuts as a staple crop early in the twentieth century. The soup is followed by another down-South favorite, a curry dish called Country Captain, which usually calls for chicken but here is made with turkey.

Menu 2 is a lighthearted brunch ideal for summer, when tomatoes and beans are at their peak. It features an appetizer of sliced country ham with papaya wedges, a variation on the Italian melon with prosciutto. The turkey hash—made with large cubes of turkey breast—contains mild Mexican chilies, a typical California touch.

For a change of pace, the cold-weather dinner of Menu 3 shows off several of the cook's favorite European recipes. She describes the first course of leeks vinaigrette as a standard French or Italian offering, while the hazelnut-coated turkey cutlets are a variation on a classic French treatment for veal or chicken.

For this popular southern meal, use a dark pottery tureen to set off the creamy peanut soup garnished with scallion greens. Before serving the Country Captain, sprinkle the top with toasted almonds and chopped parsley.

Cream of Peanut Soup
Turkey Country Captain

Food historians disagree as to whether Country Captain originated in the East Indies, the American South, or India. In any case, the dish is seasoned with curry powder—a blend of 7 to 20 different ingredients commonly used in Indian cooking. The blends of curry powder found in supermarkets are usually mild and suitable for most curry dishes. The best commercial blends, however, are imported from India and are available at specialty food shops. The aroma of curry powder deteriorates quickly if not tightly sealed and stored in a cool dark spot. To intensify its taste, cook it quickly in a small amount of fat before adding it to your recipe. For a more powerful curry flavor in this recipe, increase the quantity of powder to your taste.

WHAT TO DRINK

Offer a slightly fruity white wine or a light red with this menu. For white, try a dry California Chenin Blanc or a New York State Riesling; for red, choose a young Italian Dolcetto or a California Gamay Beaujolais.

SHOPPING LIST AND STAPLES

1½-pound section of boneless, skinless turkey breast
4 medium-size tomatoes (about 2 pounds total weight)
1 red bell pepper
1 green bell pepper
Medium-size onion
Medium-size bunch scallions
1 clove garlic
Small bunch parsley
½ pint heavy cream
3½ tablespoons unsalted butter
3 cups chicken stock, preferably homemade (see page 11), or canned
1½ tablespoons olive oil
1-pound can unsalted roasted peanuts
5½-ounce package whole almonds
9-ounce box raisins
1 tablespoon all-purpose flour
1 tablespoon curry powder
½ teaspoon dried thyme
¼ teaspoon cinnamon
¼ teaspoon ground cloves
Pinch of Cayenne pepper

Salt
Freshly ground pepper
¾ cup white wine

UTENSILS

Food processor or blender
Large heavy-gauge skillet with cover
Large saucepan
Medium-size heavy-gauge saucepan
Small baking sheet
Colander
Measuring cups and spoons
Chef's knife
Paring knife
2 wooden spoons
Slotted spoon
Rubber spatula

START-TO-FINISH STEPS

1. Follow turkey recipe steps 1 and 2.
2. Follow soup recipe steps 1 through 4.
3. While soup is simmering, follow turkey recipe steps 3 through 6.
4. While turkey is simmering, follow soup recipe steps 5 and 6, and serve as first course.
5. Follow turkey recipe steps 7 through 11, and serve.

RECIPES

Cream of Peanut Soup

Medium-size bunch scallions
2 tablespoons unsalted butter
1½ cups unsalted roasted peanuts
3 cups chicken stock
½ teaspoon salt
Freshly ground pepper
1 cup heavy cream

1. Trim scallions and rinse under cold running water; dry with paper towels. Chop enough white parts to measure ⅓ cup and enough green parts to measure 2 tablespoons. Set aside greens for garnish.
2. Heat butter in medium-size heavy-gauge saucepan over medium heat. Add white scallion parts to pan and cook, stirring occasionally, 3 minutes.

3. Transfer scallions to container of food processor fitted with steel blade or to blender. Add peanuts and ½ cup stock, and process mixture until smooth, about 1½ minutes, stopping, if necessary, to push down peanuts with rubber spatula.

4. Return peanut mixture to saucepan. Stir in remaining 2½ cups stock, ½ teaspoon salt, and pepper to taste, and simmer, uncovered, over medium heat 15 minutes, stirring occasionally.

5. Reduce heat to low and slowly add cream, stirring to blend. Cook soup over low heat just until heated through. Do not let soup boil.

6. Turn soup into tureen or bowl, sprinkle with scallion greens, and serve.

Turkey Country Captain

1½-pound section of boneless, skinless turkey
   breast
Medium-size onion
1 clove garlic
1½ tablespoons olive oil
1½ tablespoons unsalted butter
4 medium-size tomatoes (about 2 pounds total
   weight)
1 red bell pepper
1 green bell pepper
1 tablespoon all-purpose flour
1 tablespoon curry powder
½ teaspoon salt
½ teaspoon dried thyme
¼ teaspoon cinnamon
¼ teaspoon ground cloves
Pinch of Cayenne pepper
¾ cup white wine
Small bunch parsley
½ cup whole almonds
½ cup raisins

1. Bring 2 quarts of water to a boil in large saucepan over high heat.

2. Meanwhile, wash turkey and dry with paper towels. Cut turkey into ¾-inch cubes. Peel and thinly slice onion. Peel and mince garlic.

3. In large heavy-gauge skillet, heat olive oil and butter over medium-high heat. Add turkey, onion, and garlic, and cook, stirring occasionally, 8 to 10 minutes, or until turkey is slightly browned.

4. Meanwhile, plunge tomatoes into boiling water for 20 seconds. With slotted spoon, transfer tomatoes to colander and refresh under cold running water. Cut off stem ends, squeeze out seeds, and peel. Coarsely chop tomato pulp.

5. Rinse red and green bell peppers under cold running water and dry with paper towels. Halve, core, and seed peppers; cut into ¼-inch-wide strips. Preheat oven to 350 degrees.

6. Add flour, curry powder, salt, thyme, cinnamon, cloves, and Cayenne to skillet and stir to coat turkey. Stir in wine, tomatoes, and peppers. Cover skillet, reduce heat to medium-low, and simmer 20 to 25 minutes, or until turkey is tender.

7. Wash parsley, dry with paper towels, and chop enough to measure ½ cup.

8. Spread almonds on small baking sheet and toast in oven, shaking pan occasionally to prevent scorching, about 5 minutes, or until lightly browned.

9. Remove almonds from oven and set aside to cool.

10. Add raisins and ¼ cup of the parsley to turkey mixture and simmer another 5 minutes.

11. Turn Country Captain into serving dish, sprinkle with toasted almonds, and remaining ¼ cup chopped parsley, and serve.

ADDED TOUCH

This syllabub (an old-fashioned English dessert originally made with wine and fresh milk) contains orange-flavored liqueur and heavy cream and is garnished with crystallized ginger, available in most supermarkets.

Orange-Ginger Syllabub

2 tablespoons orange marmalade
2 tablespoons Grand Marnier or Cointreau
1½ cups heavy cream, chilled
Crystallized ginger for garnish

1. Place large bowl and beaters in freezer to chill.

2. Combine marmalade and liqueur in small bowl.

3. Using chilled bowl and beaters, whip cream with electric mixer at high speed until stiff.

4. Using rubber spatula, gently fold marmalade mixture into cream. Spoon syllabub into small dessert glasses or bowls, cover with plastic wrap, and chill at least 2 hours.

5. Garnish each serving with small pieces of crystallized ginger and serve.

Country Ham with Papaya and Lime
Turkey Hash with Chilies
Tomatoes with Beans and Fresh Basil

For a filling brunch, serve slices of papaya and lime on country ham, then turkey hash with a tomato and bean salad.

Country hams are salted and then smoked over a wood fire. These very flavorful hams are available whole or by the piece at some specialty butchers or by mail from producers. Here, paper thin slices of country ham are served with papaya, a sweet yellow-orange tropical fruit. A perfectly ripe papaya yields to slight pressure.

WHAT TO DRINK

With this robust menu, serve a crisp, firm white wine, such as an Italian Pinot Grigio; or offer cold beer or ale.

SHOPPING LIST AND STAPLES

1½-pound section of boneless, skinless turkey breast
½ pound country ham, thinly sliced
3 all-purpose potatoes (about 1 pound total weight)
2 medium-size tomatoes (about 1 pound total weight)
½ pound green beans, or ¼ pound plus ¼ pound wax beans
Medium-size onion

1 clove garlic
Small bunch basil
Small bunch coriander for garnish (optional)
1 lime
2 medium-size papayas or 1 large (about 1 pound)
½ pint heavy cream
4 tablespoons unsalted butter
Two 3-ounce cans whole mild green chilies
2 tablespoons white wine vinegar
6 tablespoons olive oil
3 tablespoons all-purpose flour
Salt and freshly ground black and white pepper

UTENSILS

Large ovenproof skillet
Medium-size saucepan
Large bowl
Medium-size bowl
Colander
Strainer

Measuring cups and spoons
Chef's knife
Paring knife
Wooden spoon
Metal spatula
Vegetable peeler

START-TO-FINISH STEPS

1. Wash basil, and coriander if using, and dry with paper towels. Finely shred enough basil leaves to measure 2 tablespoons for tomatoes recipe. Mince enough coriander to measure 2 tablespoons for hash recipe.
2. Follow hash recipe steps 1 through 4.
3. While hash is browning, follow tomatoes recipe steps 1 through 5.
4. Follow hash recipe step 5.
5. While sauce is thickening, follow ham recipe steps 1 through 3.
6. Follow hash recipe step 6, and serve ham and papaya as first course.
7. Follow hash recipe step 7 and serve with tomatoes.

RECIPES

Country Ham with Papaya and Lime

2 medium-size papayas or 1 large (about 1 pound)
1 lime
½ pound country ham, thinly sliced
Freshly ground black pepper

1. Peel papayas, cut in half, and scoop out seeds; slice flesh into 12 wedges.
2. Wash lime and dry with paper towels. Cut into twelve ⅛-inch-thick slices.
3. Divide ham equally among salad plates and top with alternating wedges of papaya and slices of lime. Sprinkle with freshly ground black pepper.

Turkey Hash with Chilies

1½-pound section of boneless, skinless turkey breast
3 all-purpose potatoes (about 1 pound total weight)
Medium-size onion
1 clove garlic
3 tablespoons all-purpose flour
4 tablespoons unsalted butter
1 cup heavy cream
Two 3-ounce cans whole mild green chilies
Salt and freshly ground white pepper
2 tablespoons minced coriander for garnish (optional)

1. Preheat oven to 200 degrees.
2. Wash turkey and dry with paper towels. Cut turkey into ¾-inch cubes. Wash potatoes, peel, and cut into ¾-inch cubes. Peel and dice onion. Peel and mince garlic.
3. Place flour in medium-size bowl. Add turkey cubes and toss to coat thoroughly. Shake off any excess flour.
4. Heat butter in large ovenproof skillet over medium-high heat just until melted. Add turkey, potatoes, onion,

and garlic, and cook, stirring with wooden spoon, until turkey loses its pink color, 4 to 5 minutes. Continue cooking another 15 minutes, turning with spatula every 5 minutes, until turkey and potatoes brown.
5. Stir in cream, reduce heat to medium-low, and cook 5 to 10 minutes, or until turkey and potatoes are tender and sauce has thickened.
6. Turn chilies into strainer and drain. Rinse under cold running water and dry. Cut chilies into 2-inch-long strips and add to skillet. Add salt and pepper to taste; place skillet in oven until ready to serve.
7. Divide hash among 4 dinner plates and garnish each serving with coriander, if desired.

Tomatoes with Beans and Fresh Basil

½ pound green beans, or ¼ pound plus ¼ pound wax beans
2 medium-size tomatoes (about 1 pound total weight)
2 tablespoons white wine vinegar
6 tablespoons olive oil
Salt and freshly ground black pepper
2 tablespoons finely shredded basil

1. In medium-size saucepan, bring 1½ quarts water to a boil over high heat.
2. Meanwhile, wash beans under cold running water. Trim off ends of beans. Add beans to boiling water and cook 5 to 7 minutes, or just until tender.
3. While beans are cooking, wash tomatoes and dry with paper towels. Core tomatoes and cut into wedges.
4. Turn beans into colander, refresh under cold running water, and drain.
5. In large bowl, combine tomatoes and beans. Sprinkle with vinegar, oil, and salt and pepper to taste, and toss to combine. Sprinkle with basil and set aside until ready to serve.

ADDED TOUCH

Grits are made from dried, hulled white or yellow corn kernels called hominy. White grits are preferred here.

Cheese Grits

¾ cup white hominy grits
¼ teaspoon salt, approximately
¼ pound Cheddar cheese
¼ cup heavy cream
4 tablespoons unsalted butter, cut into pieces
Freshly ground white pepper

1. In medium-size saucepan, bring 3½ cups water to a boil over high heat. Reduce heat to medium and stir grits slowly into water. Add salt and return mixture to a boil. Reduce heat until grits are barely simmering, cover, and cook, stirring occasionally, 25 to 30 minutes.
2. While grits are cooking, grate cheese to measure 1 cup.
3. Stir cheese, cream, and butter into grits. Cook over low heat, stirring, until cheese melts.
4. Season to taste with salt and pepper, and serve.

Leeks Vinaigrette with Feta Cheese and Black Olives
Hazelnut Turkey Cutlets
Carrot and Zucchini Sauté

Hazelnut turkey cutlets, sautéed carrots and zucchini, and leeks with olives and feta cheese are an elegant but easy meal.

Sautéed turkey cutlets with a hazelnut and bread crumb crust make a sumptuous entrée. To ensure that the coating sticks to the meat, dust each cutlet thoroughly with flour before dipping it into the beaten egg mixture and then into the nuts and crumbs. The coating seals in the meat juices while forming a crunchy exterior.

Leeks look like very large scallions and are prized for their sweet, delicate flavor. Select straight leeks of uniform size with crisp green leaves. Avoid any with bulbous bottoms because these are usually tough and woody. When leeks are cooked, the white part will be tender but still slightly resistant when pierced with the point of a knife.

Crumbled feta cheese and Niçoise olives are sprinkled over the leeks before serving. Greek feta cheese is salty, with a sharp taste. It usually comes in brine-filled trays by the piece at cheese shops and most supermarkets. Brine-cured Niçoise olives from Provence range in color from brown to purple to black and are packed in herb-flavored olive oil. As a substitute, use any oil-packed olives from Italy or Greece.

WHAT TO DRINK

A full-bodied, fruity white wine would go best with the varied flavors and textures of this meal. The best choice would be a moderately priced California Chardonnay. As a good alternative, you might want to purchase either a French Mâcon or a simple Chablis.

SHOPPING LIST AND STAPLES

Four ½-inch-thick turkey cutlets (about 1 pound total weight)
4 or 5 medium-size carrots (about 1 pound total weight)
2 medium-size zucchini (about ¾ pound total weight)
8 small leeks (about 1½ pounds total weight)
Small clove garlic
Small bunch parsley
Small bunch dill or parsley
1 lemon
2 eggs
1 stick unsalted butter
¼ pound feta cheese
7-ounce jar imported small black olives, preferably Niçoise
1 tablespoon Dijon mustard
3 tablespoons red wine vinegar
½ cup plus 2 tablespoons olive oil
5½-ounce package shelled hazelnuts, preferably, or walnuts
½ cup all-purpose flour
¾ cup dry bread crumbs
Salt
Freshly ground black pepper
½ cup dry white wine

UTENSILS

Food processor (optional)
Large heavy-gauge skillet
Medium-size heavy-gauge skillet with cover
Large saucepan
15 x 10-inch baking sheet
Pie plate
Ovenproof serving platter
Small bowl
Colander
Measuring cups and spoons
Chef's knife
Paring knife
Wooden spoon
Metal spatula
Small whisk
Vegetable peeler
Grater (if not using processor)
Mallet or rolling pin
Kitchen string

START-TO-FINISH STEPS

1. Follow leeks recipe step 1.
2. Follow turkey recipe steps 1 through 4.
3. Follow leeks recipe steps 2 through 6.
4. Follow carrots recipe steps 1 and 2.
5. Follow turkey recipe steps 5 and 6.
6. As second batch of turkey is cooking, follow carrots recipe step 3.
7. Follow turkey recipe step 7 and carrots recipe step 4.
8. Follow turkey recipe step 8, leeks recipe step 7, and serve with carrots.

RECIPES

Leeks Vinaigrette with Feta Cheese and Black Olives

8 small leeks (about 1½ pounds total weight)
¼ pound feta cheese
Small clove garlic
1 tablespoon Dijon mustard
3 tablespoons red wine vinegar
Salt
Freshly ground black pepper
6 tablespoons olive oil
¼ cup imported small black olives, preferably Niçoise

1. In large saucepan, bring 2 quarts of water to a boil over high heat.
2. Trim off ends of leeks and discard. Split each leek lengthwise from top to within 2 to 3 inches of root end, taking care not to cut completely through leek. Spread leaves apart and rinse leeks thoroughly under cold running water to remove all grit.
3. Tie leeks together with kitchen string. Lower them into rapidly boiling water and cook, uncovered, over high

heat, 5 to 7 minutes, or just until tender when tested with point of small sharp knife.

4. While leeks are cooking, crumble enough feta cheese to measure ½ cup. Peel garlic and mince enough to measure ½ teaspoon.

5. In small bowl, combine garlic, mustard, vinegar, and salt and pepper to taste and whisk until blended. Still whisking, add olive oil in a slow, steady stream and whisk until dressing is thick and smooth.

6. Transfer leeks to colander and immediately refresh under cold running water. Untie bundle and arrange leeks in single layer in shallow serving dish. Pour half of dressing over leeks and place remaining dressing in small serving pitcher or bowl. Set leeks and dressing aside.

7. Just before serving, sprinkle leeks with feta cheese and olives. Serve with vinaigrette on the side.

Hazelnut Turkey Cutlets

¾ cup hazelnuts, preferably, or walnuts
¾ cup dry bread crumbs
½ cup all-purpose flour
Salt and freshly ground black pepper
2 eggs
Four ½-inch-thick turkey cutlets (about 1 pound
    total weight)
Small bunch parsley
4 tablespoons olive oil
4 tablespoons unsalted butter
½ cup dry white wine

1. Using food processor fitted with steel blade, or chef's knife, finely chop nuts.

2. Combine nuts with bread crumbs on sheet of waxed paper. On second sheet of waxed paper, combine flour with salt and pepper to taste. Break eggs into pie plate and beat with 1 tablespoon water until blended.

3. Place turkey cutlets between 2 more sheets of waxed paper and pound to ¼-inch-thickness with mallet or rolling pin. If cutlets are large, cut each in half.

4. Dip each turkey cutlet into flour and gently shake off excess. Dip into eggs and then into nut mixture, gently pressing to help coating adhere. Arrange cutlets in single layer on baking sheet, cover with plastic wrap, and refrigerate at least 20 minutes to set coating.

5. Wash parsley and dry with paper towels. Mince enough parsley to measure ¼ cup.

6. Preheat oven to 200 degrees. In large heavy-gauge skillet, heat olive oil and butter over medium-high heat. When butter foams, add only as many cutlets to skillet as will fit without crowding and sauté 3 to 4 minutes per side, or until lightly browned. As they are cooked, transfer cutlets to ovenproof serving platter and keep warm in oven. Repeat for remaining cutlets.

7. Add wine to skillet and cook over high heat, scraping up any brown bits clinging to bottom of pan with wooden spoon, about 3 minutes, or until sauce is reduced to about ¼ cup.

8. Stir minced parsley into sauce and pour over cutlets.

Carrot and Zucchini Sauté

4 or 5 medium-size carrots (about 1 pound total weight)
2 medium-size zucchini (about ¾ pound total weight)
Small bunch dill or parsley
1 lemon
4 tablespoons unsalted butter
Salt
Freshly ground black pepper

1. Wash, trim, and peel carrots. Wash zucchini and dry with paper towels. Trim off ends and discard. Shred carrots and zucchini in food processor fitted with shredding disk, or on coarse side of grater.

2. Wash dill or parsley, dry with paper towels, and chop enough to measure ¼ cup. Squeeze enough lemon juice to measure 2 tablespoons.

3. In medium-size heavy-gauge skillet, melt butter over medium heat. Add carrots and zucchini and sauté, stirring occasionally, until just tender but still slightly crunchy, about 6 minutes.

4. Season vegetables with salt and pepper to taste. Stir in dill or parsley and lemon juice. Remove pan from heat, cover, and keep warm until ready to serve.

━━━━━━━━━
ADDED TOUCH

Although traditionally served in small, lidded porcelain pots, this dessert could also be presented in demitasse cups.

Chocolate Pots de Crème

½ cup heavy cream (optional)
¼ pound sweet chocolate
¾ cup half-and-half or light cream
2 tablespoons sugar
3 eggs
1 tablespoon dark rum
½ teaspoon vanilla extract

1. If using heavy cream, place bowl and beaters in freezer to chill.

2. Combine chocolate, half and half or light cream, and sugar in small heavy-gauge saucepan and cook over low heat, stirring occasionally, about 5 minutes, or until chocolate is melted.

3. Meanwhile, separate eggs, reserving whites for another use.

4. Remove pan from heat and beat in egg yolks, one at a time. Stir in rum and vanilla extract.

5. Return pan to low heat and cook 2 to 3 minutes, or until mixture begins to thicken.

6. Pour chocolate cream into 4 demitasse cups or small soufflé dishes, cover, and place in refrigerator to chill several hours.

7. If using heavy cream, whip in chilled bowl with chilled beaters until stiff.

8. Top each pot de crème with a spoonful of whipped cream, if using, and serve.

Acknowledgments

The Editors would like to thank the following for their courtesy in lending items for photography: *Cover:* plate—ceramic designer Claire Des Becker. *Frontispiece:* marble, pan—Pottery Barn; knife—J. A. Henckels Zwillingswerk, Inc.; stove—Tappan. *Pages 16–17:* tiles—Country Floors, Inc.; platter, bowl—Ad Hoc Housewares. *Page 20:* fork—The Lauffer Co.; frog—Five Eggs; coaster, plate, napkin, spoon—Ad Hoc Housewares. *Page 23:* plate—Julien Mousa-Oghli; condiment dishes, utensils—The Museum Store of The Museum of Modern Art; tiles—Country Floors, Inc. *Pages 26–27:* boards—Bowl & Board; casserole—Mad Monk; tablecloth—China Seas. *Page 30:* plate—Terrafirma, Inc.; tablecloth—Conran's. *Page 33:* plates—Dan Bleier; utensils, glass—Gorham. *Pages 36–37:* utensils—Gorham; glasses, carafe—Saint Louis; platters, dishes—Robert Haviland & C. Parlon. *Page 40:* plates—Julien Mousa-Oghli; tablecloth, glasses—Conran's; bowl, spoon—Charles Lamalle; fork, knife—Wallace Silversmiths. *Page 46–47:* plate, bowl, chopsticks, chopstick rest—Sointu; spoon—The Lauffer Co.; orchids courtesy of Mrs. Lucille Maffei. *Page 50:* tablecloth—Peter Fasano; glass—Gorham. *Page 53:* platters—Barbara Eigen; rug—Bowl & Board; servers—Gorham. *Pages 56–57:* utensils—Gorham; tablecloth—Conran's; napkins—The Lauffer Co. *Page 60:* plates—Mad Monk; napkin—Conran's. *Pages 64–65:* utensils—Gorham; tablecloth, glass, dishes, napkin—Pierre Deux. *Pages 68–69:* plates—Dan Bleier; napkin—Conran's. *Page 71:* plate, glass—Haviland & Co.; utensils—Wallace Silversmiths; tablecloth—Pierre Deux. *Pages 74–75:* tureen, platter—Louis Lourioux; wooden bowl—Bowl & Board. *Page 78:* vase, dishes—Conran's; utensils—Wallace Silversmiths. *Page 81:* platter, casserole—Conran's. *Pages 84–85:* rug, salad bowl—Pan American Phoenix; cheese bowl—Conran's. *Page 88:* plates—Wolfman-Gold & Good Co.; napkins—Ad Hoc Housewares; tablecloth—Conran's. *Page 91:* platter, tablecloth—Conran's; servers—The Lauffer Co.; salad bowl—Ad Hoc Housewares. *Pages 94–95:* soup bowls—Conran's; tureen, platter—Mud Sweat & Tears, Inc. *Page 98:* dishes—Franciscan by Wedgwood; napkin—Leacock & Co.; tablecloth—Conran's. *Page 100:* platters—Haviland & Co.; servers—Gorham. *Kitchen equipment courtesy of:* White-Westinghouse, Commercial Aluminum Cookware Co., Robot-Coupe, Caloric, Kitchen-Aid, J.A. Henckels Zwillingswerk, Inc., and Schwabel Corp. Microwave oven compliments of Litton Microwave Cooking Products.

Illustrations by Ray Skibinski
Production by Giga Communications

Mail-Order Sources for Andouille

Cajun King Smokehouse
310 Silbert Street
Oakland, CA 94608

Oak Grove Smokehouse
17618 Old Jefferson Highway
Prairieville, LA 70769

Index

103

*Time-Life Books Inc. offers a wide
range of fine recordings, including
a Big Band series. For subscription
information, call 1-800-621-7026, or
write TIME-LIFE MUSIC, Time & Life
Building, Chicago, Illinois 60611.*